WILMA ELLERSIEK

GESTURE GAMES FOR AUTUMN AND WINTER

Hand Gesture Games, Songs and Movement Games
for Children in Kindergarten and the Lower Grades

TRANSLATED AND EDITED BY
LYN AND KUNDRY WILLWERTH

WITH CONTRIBUTIONS BY
MARGRET COSTANTINI AND
ELEANOR WINSHIP

WALDORF EARLY CHILDHOOD ASSOCIATION OF NORTH AMERICA

Acknowledgments

This publication was made possible by a grant from the Waldorf Curriculum Fund. The first editions of the original German texts were published under the title, *Handgestenspiele, Reigen und Lieder* by Wilma Ellersiek, Verlag Freies Geistesleben & Urachhaus, Stuttgart. copyright © Verlag Freies Geistesleben & Urachhaus, GmbH, Stuttgart, Germany, 2002.

This English edition contains most of the material from the German edition, selected, edited and translated by Kundry and Lyn Willwerth.

This edited English translation copyright © Waldorf Early Childhood Association of North America, 2007.

Published by
Waldorf Early Childhood Association of North America (WECAN)
285 Hungry Hollow Road, Spring Valley, New York 10977 USA.

ISBN: 978-0-9722238-9-8

10 9 8 7 6 5 4 3 2 1

Illustration and cover: Friedericke Lögters
Musical notations: Ingrid Weidenfeld
Design and typeset: Roland Willwerth
Copy editor: Barbara Audley
Printed by: Alphagraphics, Pittsburgh, PA, USA

TABLE OF CONTENTS

INTRODUCTION

Translators' Foreword

This collection of gesture games for the autumn and winter complete the cycle of games for the course of the year. Dramatic changes in nature are taking place in the fall, as the summer's fruit matures and is ready for harvest, the trees change their color and the first frost touches plants and flowers around us. In the moving and touching games of this book we can experience the blowing of the autumn wind, the fog hanging in the air and the earth getting ready for winter.

But as it becomes quiet, cold and snow-covered outside, Wilma Ellersiek shows us in her games how much fun and enjoyment the winter can bring, building a snowman, skating and sledding, watching the animals in their winter activities. Some of our best-beloved festivals fall in this season and Wilma Ellersiek offers us songs and games to help celebrate harvest festivals, Halloween and Christmas. This is a book full of joyful activities, but also of inner contemplation to help you celebrate the course of the year with your children.

Those of the children lucky enough to play together for a second or third year are already looking forward to familiar games. Will the wind blow again through the yard, making the fallen leaves dance and twirl, swing and turn, down to the earth in a big heap? Will the fog hide the world in his big, dense mantle, making us grope our way along, hardly able to see? Will we skate again on the lake with our make-believe skates, gliding on the ice, turning in a pirouette and – whoops! – tumble and fall? Each year we can play it better, form the gestures more plastically, join more strongly in the melody of speech and song. We open our eyes and hearts to the rushing of the wind, the "plop" of the falling apple, the rustle of the dry leaves, the stillness of the falling snowflakes. With gratitude we experience the mysteries of nature, uniting ourselves with them in play. And we are thankful that Wilma Ellersiek could create these wonderful games, so that we can be part of the working of nature through play.

In rendering these plays in English we hope that you, dear reader, will be drawn into this experience. It will take preparation, learning the games in word and gestures so that your children can join in the playing. It may be difficult, at the onset, to combine word and gestures harmoniously. But how rewarding is the effort, when we see the children's enthusiasm in playing with us! And with each game it becomes easier to learn a new one.

We wish you and your children joy in your work with this book!

We also thank Margret Costantini, who gives us such a clear description of how Wilma Ellersiek's games have been created. Thanks also to Eleanor Winship, who helps us "find a tonal doorway" into the world of the young child, opens our understanding to the simple mood-of-the-fifth songs that are part of these games. Thus, she helps us to appreciate the mood of the open fifth and its connection to nature and the cosmos.

One festival of autumn, Halloween, is celebrated primarily in Britain and America. However, this fall festival has a corresponding early spring festival on the European continent: Mardi Gras or "Fasching." Both festivals are celebrated by taking on a different character through costume change, trickery and fun. With Wilma Ellersiek's permission we have changed the "Fasching" song into a Halloween song and hope you will enjoy it in this "American" form.

As with the other two collections of games by Wilma Ellersiek, Hillside Kindergarten offers a CD of the songs contained in this book. This is not a new CD, but instead the autumn and winter songs of this volume were recorded together with the songs for spring and summer, so that the music of both books are sung for you on the CD: *Gesture Games for Spring and Summer, Autumn and Winter.*

To help singers with low voices, an alternative to the singing of the high E is offered in the song: *All the Things Autumn Can Do.* Here the alternative setting, one fifth below the printed notes, is the only melody recorded.

Singers are encouraged to make every effort to use the original setting of the songs. This will foster the development of musicality in young children as they cannot yet clearly distinguish low notes.

Creating Rhythmic-Musical Games

All of the rhythmic, musically formed games in this book reveal nature to the attentive listener. It is necessary to carefully observe and understand the world and to find out, rather than to invent. Everything is already there; we only need to sensitize our perceptions by holding back our feelings and opinions, approaching the phenomena selflessly, open to what they have to say to us. They reveal their secrets only to the selfless mind; only in this way is their open secret perceptible.

With a devoted heart we must mold artistically, creatively, according to the children's needs, what was discovered in the powerful realm of nature. That means finding the fitting gesture that will give voice to what nature presents and forming speech in a musically-rhythmic way. The speech gesture must be discovered and formed so as to coincide with the movement. Image and observation of speech are not valid here, since they lead into mind and thought activity. It is the child's will-force that must be addressed, and that happens only through bearing and gesture. The sequence of movement itself is the basis, the primal form of the concept and of human behavior.

This is true for anything: movement, language, speech, speaking and singing, noises, sounds and tones. It is also true in transmitting the spoken or sung gesture games to sound or tone-giving instruments. These must be integrated into the games, never abstractly, but always together with the movement, as "playmates."

Most importantly, adults educating children must concern themselves intensively and selflessly with these situations, and with strength of ego, pass them on to the children. They must practice long and hard: their gestures, their speech, their voices, also their use of the sounding and basic instruments. All these must be perfected, so as to make possible, in their actions, a high quality offering the children can imitate. This can provide them with food for building their bodily organisms and as a help for their incarnation.

All natural occurences embodied in gestures as example or archetype are given the possibility to be physically perceived and repeated by the children, either with or in imitation of the hand or body gesture. Through this they discover something of the truth, of the essential form of the appearance, making it their own through imitation. They win a bodily knowledge of the world, of creation, and, fed by this spirit-substance, build their organisms, laying the physical foundation for clear thought and knowledge of spiritual truth.

The development of the game, with equally stressed alternation of movement and rest, of hand movement and movement in space, follows from the natural order, the habits of the animals in the various living realms. This measure of fullness is enough, no more is needed, since the entire course of the game, through poetic speech, is already a thoroughly musical and rhythmic event. And speech, in the child's first seven years, presents in the very best way a musical experience; it stands in first place.

The tonal variations in rhythmic-melodious speaking and the richness of varying rhythms in poetic speech, as well as in these artistically formed speech-games stressing tone, syllable and sound is unprecedented. This is as true for exercising the organs of speech and voice as for the imaginative use of language. Likewise, the children feel this rhythmic-melodious speaking as music. "Sing it again!" they say when begging for a speech game to be repeated. That is especially the case for the so-called "nonsense" word sequences of tone, syllable and sounds. They are without exception, felt by all children up to school age and beyond as a musical event.

This purely spiritual-feeling substance of speech, as yet untouched by the intellect, is a refreshing bath and at the same time nourishing food that the child of this stage of life happily receives. This artistic presentation of tone and syllables has nothing to so with so-called "baby talk" that adults sometimes unfortunately use to the disadvantage of the child. In the first seven years, speech, together with movement and singing, is the link to musicality. "Parsed" musicality and abstracted rhythm are not yet present. This analysis into separate realms of musical experience begins only shortly before entry into school. And then the rhythmic patterns are still quite simple. A double beat dominates almost entirely; even in singing mode, a triple beat seldom appears.

The children perceive fixed intonation, but mostly, they cannot produce it exactly. Harmonies (chords) are not yet heard; the children are, as it were, "deaf" to them. On the other hand, they can experience the richness of sound in speech and the rhythmic variety in movement. The raptness with which children in this stage of development imitate speech and hand gesture games, song and circle games (spatial movement games), or play such games just for themselves, shows the connection between movement, speech and singing to be a suitable form of music-making for children of this age.

In view of this fact, the introduction of instruments needs to be very carefully considered. To diverge too early into the use of instruments does not fit the needs of the child's inner being and does not enrich, but in this phase actually impoverishes within the sphere of musicality. If the inclusion of musical rhythm-instruments is desired for noise, sound or tone production, one can invite them as "play-mates," integrating them into the course of the game. This "play-mate" does what we do, or tells about itself; the children play along, copying what it does.

For young children, either in the family or in kindergarten, rhythmic-musical speaking and singing are appropriate. Of course, a great deal of patience is needed to be able to use your speaking or singing voice so that it has the effect of a musical instrument. To speak in a rhythmically-musical way, the rhythm and melody patterns of speech need to be emphasized. The movement and sound of speech are in the foreground, whereas content, meaning and concept are secondary. Singing is instrumental, an objective event of sound, unsentimental; the content of one's own feelings are suppressed.

The sculpture of sounds, the gesture of the words, the rhythmic-pulse in the flow of speech, the melodious tone, the multifaceted tone-coloring, the differentiation in the tone dynamics, all need to be given attention when rehearsing. It is a speaking activity that approaches song, removed from the prosaic. The third-interval, so common when calling someone, is to be avoided, as it engenders an unwanted stereotypical speech-melody. Instead, the tone of the words follows the habit of language itself. This way, a tonal dynamic and diversity can be achieved that defies any system of notation. In this way, the child enjoys a richness of tonality and a diversity of sound, an objectively musical experience without drama.

In this way, the creative, artistic essence of speech stands in the foreground, and not the conceptual content. The child experiences and lives immersed in the process of sound formation and in helping to produce the character of the words, in the essence of language, in its original gesture, or movement, and not in its abstracted concepts. The child can entirely incorporate the language for him or herself and find in this way complete, profound spiritual acculturation. Speech and language as presented here have creative functions. They mold the organism of the child and form the basis for creative, imaginative play with language.

Margret Costantini

FINDING THE TONAL DOORWAY TO EARLY CHILDHOOD

The English-speaking world has long needed a book such as this. We have here a treasure of rhythmic, musical gesture games for the young child. Its simplicity is a hard-achieved triumph, as it springs out of a profound understanding both of art and of early childhood. Wilma Ellersiek is a fine musician who has entered into the imagination and rhythm of these words and pictures and created beautiful songs and verses for the fall and winter. The hand gestures are magical – very simple and most satisfying for an adult to do with children.

On a personal note, I remember the looks on my own children's faces when we visited Kundry Willwerth's kindergarten years ago, and she did some of these songs with them. The mood was hushed, eyes were wide open and the children were captivated. These songs and words touch upon the pulse of early childhood. They are subtle and flowing – similar to the very same rhythms in nature. Nowhere here do you find the clickety clack of a train on a track – that would be a more regular and mechanical rhythm, and not to be found in nature. The music is un-metered and flows like a breeze through the fall leaves or the snow gently floating down to earth.

These flowing rhythms surround the child with a sense of well-being – you can feel this when you try them with children. There is almost a palpable sense of a quiet outbreath – a relaxed and peaceful attunement. There is nothing forced or artificial about that quality. These words and songs are anything but sentimental and need to be sung in an objectively quiet and peaceful way.

The melodies ask to be sung with a pure and gentle tone (the less vibrato the better.) Best is to sing clearly and simply on your breath stream, not pushing the tone, so that the child is surrounded by a dome of tone. The melodies are tuned to the tone A, and it might be helpful to have an instrument such as a children's harp or flute or tone bar to ring the A and then hum it before you begin.

The songs are all in the "mood of the fifth," which Rudolf Steiner advocated as the ideal musical mode for early childhood.

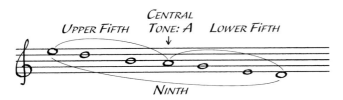

Pentatonic mood of the fifth
(original ancient Greek form) with central tone A

The tones hover around A, moving up a step to B or down to G, but keeping A as the center. There are no half steps in this pentatonic scale and this alleviates the sense of tension that half steps introduce into music. From A, we then move up to B, D and E, and then from A, the tones are likewise mirrored downwards to G, E and D.

Choosing these tones without the smaller half steps and remaining centered on A keeps us hovering without major or minor inclinations. The songs don't end with a sense of having come home to the earth on the tonic. Mood of the fifth music stays floating in the realm of early childhood – still intuitively connected to the cosmos and nature. Similar to medieval chant, which also floats, the melodies waft as gently as a breeze, while the rhythms are also not yet "of this world."

How do you enter into this "mood of the fifth?" I recommend taking a few moments of peace and quiet, perhaps early in the morning or at sunset (I turn off lights and sit on my bed or near the window) and take an instrument: harp or flute (whatever you play) and simply play the fifth interval using the notes A and E a few times. Let the tones ring. Then play the fourth interval with the notes A and D several times. Dream into the sounds and feel the mood these tones create. Then using A as your central tone, play up and down a bit while surrounding the A with the pentatonic tones described above, always returning to A. It may take a while to feel your way into this new – but ancient – "mood of the fifth." This is the opening into the child's musical language – a world still attuned to the flow of the natural world. It takes a quiet, meditative approach to begin to enter the mystery of the child's world. The songs and melodies in this book in their quiet and subtle way open a door into this world.

Eleanor Winship

PREFACE

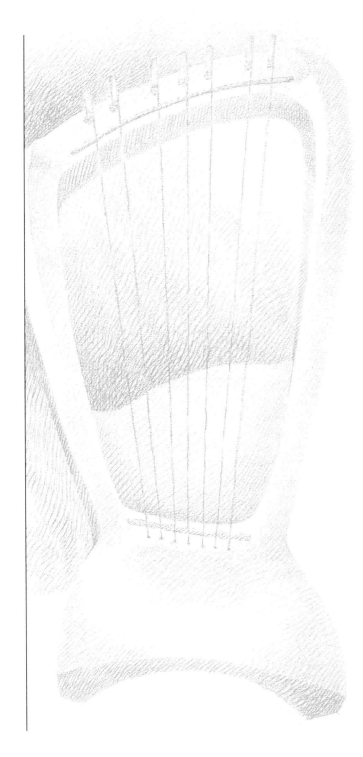

The Basic Choroi Instruments

The tonal quality of Choroi instruments corresponds to the constitutional needs of children from birth to seven years and also to the needs of handicapped or sick children. The paucity of overtones and weak resonance of sound does not attack the loose bodily organization of children and does not enter too strongly into their soul's conformation. The sound remains on the outside and wafts about like a breath of air caressing the child. It becomes a protective cloak into which the child can cuddle.

Any shrill or strong sound or tone wakes the children too much. It may in fact even frighten them and cause them damage. It has often be noticed that, during play, children do not really settle down if, for example, a powerfully sounding C-recorder with its many overtones is played. Instead of genuine release and exhalation, the children only pretend to rest.

The Choroi Flutes

These are very suitable by reason of their diffuse, not quite directly resolved tone and their weakness of resonance and overtones. The tender tone, wafting like a soft breath of air, is like a caress to the child, feeling good, not distressing.

A good preparation for developing tone that flows on the stream of breath is to play the Choroi interval flute, interval D-A. This pearwood flute with but one finger-hole can be played without any special technical difficulty, since to play both notes, D and A, only the tip of the right index finger is either laid upon or raised from the single hole. Thus one can concentrate on the use of the breath. (This flute can also be played by children shortly before their entry into first grade.

There is no "tonguing" in beginning a note, one only whispers "hooooh" into the flute, while forming through the breath various dynamics of tone strength. The continuity of the breath should not be broken while laying on or removing the fingertip.

Who has not yet mastered playing the Choroi flute so that the tone glides upon the breath, should rather sing or hum, until the desired tone quality can be achieved. Still, it is desirable to also let the flute sound for the children.

The Choroi Kinderharp

The sound of the kinderharp has a decidedly floating character. Built without any resonance box, the resulting sound is weak in resonance and overtones, a tone quality which approaches the children like a breath of air. The seven strings of the kinderharp are tuned to the notes of the "mood of the fifth." The middle string is the central tone A. This instrument particularly emphasizes the balance of the mood of the fifth through the arrangement of the strings.

The floating tone sounds through the surrounding space, swings toward the listener as a breath of air, without settling down and without penetrating the children's still loosely constructed organization. It does not invade, only enfolds; calls forth the readiness to cuddle into this cloak of sound, then to expand into the liberating, open space and unburdened, to breath freely.

Manner of Playing

The playing technique plays an important role for achieving the desired tone quality. The foot of the harp is set upon the player's left thigh. The player's left hand loosely holds the wooden post of the instrument nearest the knee, so that the harp lies upon the left lower arm of the player. The player's right plucks the strings. Single tones are plucked without pulling the strings. To draw the tone out longer, one raises one's hand in an arc away from the strings, then returns it to the instrument.

General Remarks on Notation

The central tone A referred to is the A above middle C. The notes do not represent fixed note values based on measurable time lengths. They are meant as memory aids for the melodies. Sing freely, following the motion of language and movement, not being necessarily bound by long or short notes or time-beat. The flow of speech determines the rhythmic and dynamic movement. ● ≈ a basic unit: the pulsation oriented to the heartbeat, in the streaming, swinging musical flow, without a time-beat indicated by stress or firmly bound to note length.

Singing should follow the rhythm of speech, calm, possibly slowing at the end. In playing instruments as well, follow a free rhythm in the melodies, giving emphasis where the text asks for it.

The tempo, whether sung or played on an instrument, is determined not only by the song's character, but also depends on the situation in which it is sung or played. If previous play has been lively, start by picking up the song somewhat faster, gradually leading into a calm mood. If already calm, one can start slower. With restless or nervous children, a faster basic tempo is needed than for calm natured children. Parents and care-givers must develop a fine sensibility in order to accommodate each individual situation or possibility. That means: practice — practice — practice!

In the singing of lullabies to a child in the first seven years the same holds true as in the rest of life. Parents and caregivers must above all prepare themselves, in order to "be" that which they want to present to the children. Then the child can imitate and breathe along with that which leads to calmness. We need to be aware of, and should joyfully accept, our responsibility. Having the children become, to use the Swiss folk expression "well-rocked," is well worth the effort needed on our part to develop and perfect new capacities.

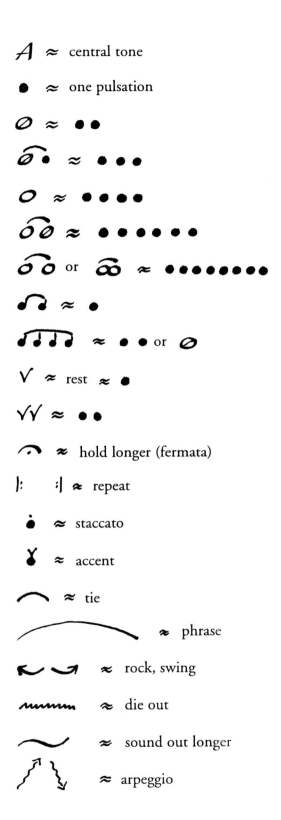

PART I: HAND GESTURE GAMES, SONGS AND MOVEMENT GAMES FOR AUTUMN

Call to St. Michael

CD track 20

Vigorous   *Text and Music: Wilma Ellersiek*

St. Mi – cha-el, oh with us be, help us batt – le, make us free!

We ask of you with us to stand while we with courage span the land!

St. Mi – cha-el, oh with us be, help us batt – le, make us free!

The sword you car – ry in your hand protecting peo-ple, sea and land.

St. Mi – cha-el, oh with us be, help us batt – le, make us free!

You call and beck – on "Follow me." You go be-fore, we fol-low thee.

St. Mi – cha-el, oh with us be, help us batt – le, make us free!

NOTATION: ● ≈ one pulsation (basic unit) in a middle tempo / √ ≈ pause of a basic pulse /
¹ ≈ short break

18

All The Things Autumn Can Do

CD track 21

HAPPY AND LIVELY   TEXT AND MELODY: WILMA ELLERSIEK

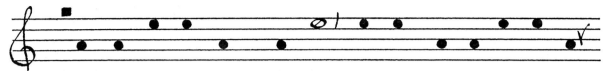

LIKE A   REAL   PAIN – TER– MAN,   AU–TUMN PAINTS THE LEAVES, HE CAN,
LIKE A   REAL   TAI – LOR – MAN,   AU–TUMN ROBES THE TREES, HE CAN,
LA – LA – LA – LA – LA – LA – LAA,   LA – LA – LA –LA – LA – LA – LA

RED   AND   YEL – LOW, BROWN AND GREEN.   WHAT A WON–DER   TO   BE   SEEN!
RED   AND   YEL – LOW, BROWN AND GREEN.   WHAT A WON–DER   TO   BE   SEEN!
RED   AND   YEL – LOW, BROWN AND GREEN.   WHAT A WON–DER   TO   BE   SEEN!

WHERE YOU LOOK, OH   WHAT   A SIGHT, ALL A–ROUND IS   MOT – LEY   BRIGHT.
WHERE YOU LOOK, BOTH   UP AND DOWN, EACH TREE WEARS A   MOT – LEY   GOWN.
WHERE YOU LOOK, OH   WHAT   A SIGHT, ALL A–ROUND IS   MOT – LEY   BRIGHT.

LIKE A   REAL   PAIN – TER– MAN,   AU–TUMN PAINTS THE LEAVES, HE CAN,
LIKE A   REAL   TAI – LOR– MAN,   AU–TUMN   ROBES THE TREES, HE CAN,
LA – LA – LA – LA – LA – LA – LAA,   LA – LA – LA – LA – LA – LA–LA

NOTATION: ● ≈ ONE PULSATION (BASIC UNIT) | ⊘ ≈ ●● | √ ≈ PAUSE OF A BASIC PULSE |
〜 ≈ SUSTAIN TONE LONGER | | ≈ SHORT BREAK ★ ≈ MELODY IN A THREE-BEAT RYTHM |
■ ≈ MELODY IN A TWO-BEAT RYTHM

TEXT:

1 Like a real painter-man,

2 Autumn paints the leaves,
he can.

3 Red and yellow, brown
a   *b*   *c*
and green,
d

HAND GESTURES:

1 Hold your lower right arm, as shown, with your loosely open hand hanging down as the "paintbrush." Your left arm and hand form a "paint can" in front of your chest. Now dip the paintbrush into the paint can and at "like a real," "stir" once, and at "painter-man," stir again, twice.

2 Silently take the paintbrush out of the can, then lightly rest your fingertips on your thumb: the paintbrush is now full of paint. Dissolve the gesture for the paint can. Now, hold your lower left arm and hand vertically, indicating the "leaf," with your palm half way tilted outward so that both you and the children can see it. With your right hand as the paintbrush, "paint" the leaf in the speech rhythm: down – up – down – up.

3 Each color has its own gesture:

a Hold your hands horizontally, with your palms up, and your fingertips turned toward the children.

b Hold your hands up, with your fingers spread and your pinkies turned toward the children.

This song can also be sung with the tones D and A. If you have trouble with the E, choose the lower fifth. The song's text can also just be spoken rhythmically without singing.

20

c Hold your hands together, pinkies touching, your lightly bent fingers toward the children. (See illustration.)

d Let your hands hang loosely down, to show a brown, wilted leaf.

4 What a wonder to be seen!

4 Shade your eyes with your hands and look to the right and left.

5 Where you look,
      ( )   *( )*
          oh what a sight,
           ( ) *( )*

5 Hold your hands and arms before your chest as if pressing a big ball against you. Your hands are not closed. Open your arms in four light, swinging movements in the speech rhythm.

6 All around is motley bright.
    V   *X*   *V*   *X*

6 Lift your hands up with fingers spread, about chest height, palms toward the children. Lightly accentuate the word "all." At "around," cross your hands; at "motley," return to the beginning hand gesture; at "bright," cross hands again.

7 Like a real painter-man,

7 As in 1.

8 Autumn paints the leaves,
             he can.

8 As in 2.

9 Like a real tailor-man,

10 Autumn robes the trees,
           he can.

11 Red and yellow,
           brown and green,
12 What a wonder to be seen!
13 Where you look,
           both up and down,
14 Each tree wears a
    V   *X*
           motley gown.
         V   *X*
15 Like a real tailor-man,
16 Autumn robes the trees,
           he can.
17 La – la – la – la – la –
   o   *o*   *o*
          la – laa,
           o
  La – la – la – la – la –
   o   *o*   *o*
          la – la.
          o

9 Hold your left hand horizontally, with loosely closed fingers in front of your chest. Your fingertips point to the right, palm down; your left hand is a piece of "fabric." Move your right pointer as a "needle" rhythmically up and down between your finger spaces. Start "sewing" at your pointer and "work" through to your pinky.

10 Lay your hands on your head. Now, at "autumn robes," stroke downward on the sides of your head to your neck and shoulders; then, at "the trees, he can," stretch your arms and hands down by your sides and so show the beautiful gown with which the autumn dresses the trees.

11 See 3, a-d.

12 See 4.
13 See 5.

14 See 6.

15 See 9.
16 See 10.

17 Turn your raised hands lightly and airily in rhythm, swinging in and out. The illustration shows your hands turned out, when you turn them in, the backs of your hands are turned toward the children.

18 Red and yellow, brown and green,	18 See 3 a-d.
19 What a wonder to be seen!	19 See 4.
20 Where you look, oh what a sight,	20 See 5.
21 All around is motley bright.	21 See 6.
22 La – la – la….	22 As in 17.

The Wind

WHEE – WHEE! HOO – HOOOO!
THE WIND! CAN YOU HEAR,
MY CHILD, MY DEAR?
WHEE – WHEE! HOO – HOOOO!
HE'S CALLING AND HE'S HOWLING TOO.
AND THEN AWAY
HE'LL QUICKLY SPRINT.
WHEE – WHEE! HOO – HOOOO!
HOO – HOOOO!
THE WIND.

TEXT:

1 Whee – whee!
        Hoo – hoooo!

2 The wind! Can you hear,

  My child, my dear?

3 Whee – whee!
        Hoo – hoooo!

4 He's calling and
        he's howling too.

HAND GESTURES:

1 With your hands, make a megaphone at your mouth and sound the call, but not too loudly. Now, touch your right ear with your right hand, bend forward a little and listen. Then speak the line:

2 Leave your right hand at your ear and listen intently. Then sit up, remove your hand from your ear, look at the children and speak the line.

3 As in 1. Increase the sound with each syllable, but don't overdo it; it has to remain musical.

4 Distinctly form all the sounds, and strongly sound the vowels.

5   And then away
    He'll quickly sprint.

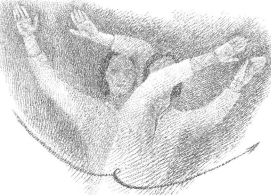

6   Whee – whee!
             Hoo – hoooo!
    Hoo – hoooo!
7   The wind.

5   Speak in a very lively way. Your arms and hands accompany the "away" and "sprint" with a lively movement that starts on the upper right side, followed by an arc, downward and outward to the left side. Raise your voice at the end and gradually let the sound die out.

6   As in 1 and 3.

7   Speak the word "the" very slowly. Then with the word "wind," repeat the arm movement in 5. Let the "w" and the "n" in wind sound strongly. Leave your voice suspended and let it die out on the "n." Text and movement of seven may be repeated.

An Apple Hangs On It

AN APPLE TREE STANDS IN MY YARD.
AN APPLE HANGS ON IT.
PHHH! – COMES THE WIND! – PHHH!
BLOWS ON IT:
PFFF! – BLOWS MORE! – PFFF! – AND MORE!
THE APPLE'S SWINGING TO AND FRO:
PFFF! – WHEE! – PFFF! – WHEE! – PFFF! – WHEE!
PLOP!
THE APPLE DROPPED.
I TAKE THE APPLE, LOOK A BIT,
THINK WHAT I COULD DO WITH IT?
CARRY IT HOME TO MOTHER QUICK.
SHE'LL MAKE APPLESAUCE OF IT:
APPLESAUCE – APPLESAUCE!
YUMM! YUMM!

TEXT:	HAND GESTURES:
1 An apple tree stands in my yard.	1 Your left arm and hand denote the apple tree. Your lower arm is the tree trunk. The palm of your hand – with spread fingers facing the children – is the branches.
2 An apple hangs on it. 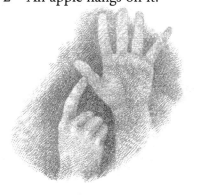	2 Your right fist is the "apple." It hangs by its stem – your right pointer – on the thickest branch – your left thumb.
3 Phhh! – comes the wind! – Phhh! Blows on it:	3 Blow lightly against the hanging apple: "phhh!"

26

4   Pfff! – blows more! – Pfff!

          – and more!

5   The apple's swinging to

          and fro:

6   Pfff! – Whee! – Pfff! –

      Whee! – Pfff! – Whee!

7   Plop!

8   The apple dropped.

9   I take the apple,

10 look a bit,
    Think what I could do
         with it.

11 Carry it home to mother

         quick

12 She'll make applesauce

        of it:

    Applesauce – applesauce!

13 Yumm! Yumm!

4   Blow more strongly against the apple: "pfff." Move the apple at the same time.

5   Show the swinging apple.

6   Continue swinging, blowing more strongly yet. At the last "whee," the apple comes loose.

7   Then the apple falls down. At the word "plop," your right fist drops onto your thigh.

8   Look attentively at the apple. Point at it with your left pointer and nod at the word "dropped."

9   Pick up the apple with your left hand and silently raise it to chest height.

10 Contemplate the apple, shaking your head and considering it.

11 Move your left hand, with the apple, in a forward, up and down rhythm, toward the children.

12 Speak the word "she" in a drawn out manner. At the same time, your left arm holds an imaginary pot and your right hand an imaginary spoon. Joyfully stir the sauce.

13 Rub your tummy with both hands, sounding a satisfied "Yumm!"

Harvest Thanksgiving
CD track 22

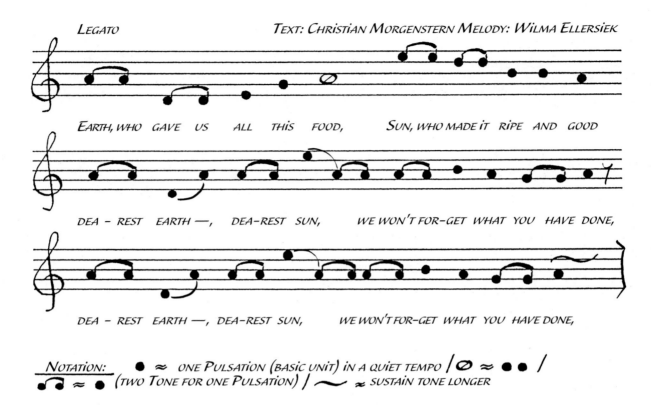

LEGATO

Text: Christian Morgenstern Melody: Wilma Ellersiek

Earth, who gave us all this food, Sun, who made it ripe and good

Dea - rest earth —, dea-rest sun, we won't for-get what you have done,

Dea - rest earth —, dea-rest sun, we won't for-get what you have done,

NOTATION: ● ≈ ONE PULSATION (BASIC UNIT) IN A QUIET TEMPO / ∅ ≈ ● ● / ♫ ≈ ● (TWO TONE FOR ONE PULSATION) / ～ ≈ SUSTAIN TONE LONGER

TEXT:

1   Earth, who gave us all
                    this food,

2   Sun, who made it ripe
                 and good,

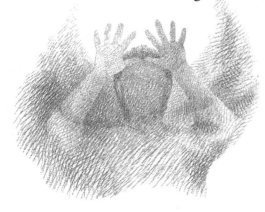

HAND GESTURES:

1   1 Raise both hands, palms up, from your thighs, the floor or the table — wherever they were resting. This expresses the growing gesture of plants.

2   Hold both hands at about forehead height, with spread fingers, and thumbs touching. The "sun" declines a bit to the front. This gesture shows the shining sun, giving warmth and light to the earth.

28

3   Dearest earth,

3   Lower both hands, palms down, and point down to the earth.

4   Dearest sun,

4   Raise your hands again, as in 2, forming the sun gesture, declining again to the front so as to let the sun shine.

5   We won't forget what you **have done.**

5   Join your hands, with fingers closed in front of your chest. Your fingertips and the balls of your hands touch, your thumbs lie between your pointers so that there is a hollow between your hands. Your hands show a "wheat ear" and also a gesture of thanks.

The Leaf

A leaf hangs on a tree,
In a dream swings she.

The wind comes tearing along.
Whee! – He tears the leaf; he's strong.
Blows her up into the air,
Hi! – She flies and dances fair.
Twirls and twirls and twirls with mirth,
Sinks at last down to the earth.

TEXT:	HAND GESTURES:

1   A leaf hangs on a tree,
    In a dream swings she.
 	
    Mm – mm – mm – mm
 	
    (Continue swinging)
	1 Hold up your right arm at chest height as a "tree limb," your right hand hangs down loosely as a "wilted leaf." Look at the leaf. At "swings," swing your hand from the wrist (see swinging arrows) while speaking softly and melodiously, almost singing. At the end, keep your voice level and let the "mm" sound out. Swing your hand two more times without speech.

2 The wind comes tearing along.	2 Speak in a very lively way. Continue the limb-leaf gesture with the right hand. Energetically move your left hand, palm directed to the right hand, from the outside to the leaf, first at "wind," then at "tearing." Speak slowly and with emphasis, almost calling. Form the sounds "w – n – t – ea – r" well and let them sound.

3   Whee! – He tears the leaf;
                    he's strong.

3   At "whee," grab the point-
    er of your right hand and
    shake it back and forth,
    holding the right hand
    very relaxed. Speak the
    word "tear" very slowly,
    so you can shake the leaf
    several times.

4   Blows her up into the air,

4   Your left hand – the wind
    – tears the right hand –
    the leaf – rhythmically up
    and down. At "up," throw
    your right hand up and let
    go of your left hand.
    Dissolve the wind gesture.
    Let your right hand, palm
    down with loose fingers,
    fly gently at head height,
    like a small parachute in
    the pattern marked at the
    right under the word "air."

5   Hi! – She flies

5   Let the leaf continue to
    float quietly according to
    the pattern marked at left.
    The speech melody, with
    higher and lower tones,
    follows the movement.
    Speak the word "flies"
    very slowly.

6   And dances fair.

6   Let the leaf, still in para-
    chute position, sink down
    to chest height, allowing it
    to circle horizontally very
    fast at the words "dances"
    and "fair." In speaking,
    keep an exact rhythm.

7   Twirls and twirls and
                    twirls with mirth,

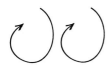

7   For twirling, turn your
    right hand palm up, like a
    little bowl, and let it sink
    to stomach height. At
    "twirls and…" swing it
    rhythmically to the right
    and left.

8 Sinks at last down to
the earth.

8 Turn your right hand back into a parachute and let the leaf slowly float down to the "earth." Speak the words "sink" and "down" very slowly, melodiously, almost singing. After the leaf has gently arrived on the earth, let it rest there for a while. (As needed, the earth, where the leaf rests, may be a table, the floor or your thighs.)

Lala – Leela – Swings The Leaflet!

WALLE – WELLE – WALLE – WELLE
FLOWS THE BROOKLET, WALLE – WELLE –

BY THE BROOKLET STANDS A TREE,
HANGING FULL OF LEAVES.

HAH!
TOOLLOOLOOLLOOLOOLLOOLOOLLOO,
DROPS A LEAF INTO THE BROOK.

LALA – LEELA, SWINGS THE LEAFLET,
LALA – LEELA, SWIMS THE LEAFLET,
ON THE WAVE INTO THE SEA.

LOOKING AFTER...
LALLALALLALALLALALLA, WAVE IT, WAVE IT ON ITS WAY.
LOOKING AFTER...
LALLALALLALALLALALLA, WAVE IT, WAVE IT ON ITS WAY.

WALLE – WELLE – WALLE – WELLE
WALLE – WELLE – WALLE – WELLE.
TULLULULLULULLULULLU
TULLULULLULULLULULLU!
LALA – LEELA – LALA – LEELA
LALA – LEELA – LALA – LEELA.
LALLALALLALALLALALLA
LALLALALLALALLALALLA!

TEXT:

1   Walle – welle – walle – welle

    Flows the brooklet,

                walle – welle –

HAND GESTURES:

1   Hold your hands above your lap, parallel to each other, to the left of your body as far as possible. With palms down, move your hands in a wave motion from left to right.

This game can also be ended with number 11. Often, children like the repetition of the syllables, particularly as speech becomes pure sound experience. All movements in 12-17 should be done very calmly and exactly.

2   By the brooklet stands a tree,

2   First point out the imaginary shore with both hands, then slowly raise your hands to form a "tree" until your arms are loosely stretched.

3   Hanging full of leaves.

3   At the word "hanging," let your hands hang loosely down.

4   Hah!

4   Look at your right, hanging hand, then say: "hah!" while the hanging hand swings toward your elbow and then bounces back.

5   Toollooloollooloollooloolloo,

     Drops a leaf into the brook.

6   Lala – leela, swings the leaflet,

5   Inconspicuously drop your left arm. Your right hand, the "leaf," spins downward in small turns as your right arm also moves downward. At the word "into," turn your hand, and at the word "brook," rest the back of your hand on your thigh.

6   Slightly lift your right hand and move it across your thigh, up and down and to and fro on imaginary waves – a figure eight, in place. Then hold your wrist and hand still.

7   Lala – leela, swims the leaflet,

     On the wave into the sea.

7   Move your right hand, palm up, in a rocking motion outward to the right. The movement is on a level plain, a brooklet, not a waterfall! Continue this movement up to the word "sea," spoken very slowly. Then point in the direction of the sea – far, far away.

8   Looking after...

9   Lallalallalallalalla, wave it,
          wave it on its way.

10   Looking after...
11   Lallalallalallalalla, wave it,
          wave it on it's way.
12   Walle – welle –
               walle – welle
     Walle – welle –
               walle – welle.
13   *silent*

14   Tullulullulullulullu
     Tullulullulullulullu!
15   Lala – leela – lala – leela
16   Lala – leela – lala – leela.

17   Lallalallalallalalla
     Lallalallalallalalla!

8   With your right hand
     above your eyes look to
     the right, to the sea.
9   Remove your right hand
     from your forehead and
     wave in the direction of
     the little leaf swimming
     away. Wave freely or on
     the speech rhythm.
10   As in 8.
11   As in 9

12   As in 1.

13   Without words, show the
     gestures of 2, 3 and 4.
14   As in 5, without the line
     of text.
15   As in 6.
16   As in 7 and 8, but
     without speaking the
     line of the text.
17   As in 9. 16 and 17 can be
     repeated.

The Wind Sends His Children About

THE WIND SENDS HIS CHILDREN ABOUT.
FROM THE WIND HOUSE THEY COME OUT.
LISTEN HERE, COULD YOU TELL ME
WHAT THIS WIND CHILD'S NAME MIGHT BE?
    SH – SH – SHSHSH,
    SH – SH – SHSHSH?

THE RUSHEL-WIND RUSHELS THE SHRUBS:
SH – SH – SHSHSH,
FIRST LOUD: SH – SH,
THEN SOFT: SHSHSH.
SO SOUNDS THE RUSHEL-WIND SONG:
SH – SH – SHSHSH!

THE WIND SENDS HIS CHILDREN ABOUT.
FROM THE WIND HOUSE THEY COME OUT.
LISTEN HERE, COULD YOU TELL ME
WHAT THIS WIND CHILD'S NAME MIGHT BE?
    P'HHH – P'HHH – P'HHH – P'HHH?

THE BLOWING-WIND BLOWS THE LEAVES FROM THE TREE:
    P'HHH – P'HHH – P'HHH – P'HHH;
AND A BEAUTIFUL DREAM HE BLOWS FOR ME:
    P'HHH – P'HHH – P'HHH – P'HHH.

THE WIND SENDS HIS CHILDREN ABOUT.
FROM THE WIND HOUSE THEY COME OUT.
LISTEN HERE, COULD YOU TELL ME
WHAT THIS WIND CHILD'S NAME MIGHT BE?
    TI – TA – TOUSLE,
    TI – TA – TOUSLE?

THE BLUSTER-WIND COMES ROARING:
    HE TI – TA – TOUSLES!
    HE TI – TA – TOUSLES!
AND OFF AGAIN SOARING!

THE WIND SENDS HIS CHILDREN ABOUT.

FROM THE WIND HOUSE THEY COME OUT.

LISTEN HERE, COULD YOU TELL ME

WHAT THIS WIND CHILD'S NAME MIGHT BE?

    WHEE – WHEE – RRRRRR –

    WHEE – WHEE – RRRRRR?

THE WHIRLY-WIND, HE WHIRLS AROUND:

    WHEE – WHEE – WHIRL ABOUT;

    WHEE – WHEE – A WHIRLING BLAST;

    WHEE – WHEE – TURNS SO FAST!

THE WIND SENDS HIS CHILDREN ABOUT.

FROM THE WIND HOUSE THEY COME OUT.

LISTEN HERE, CAN YOU TELL ME

WHAT THIS WIND CHILD'S NAME MIGHT BE?

    SOOOO – SOOOO –

    SOOOO – SOOOO?

THE SWAYING-WIND, HE SOUGHS AND SINGS:

    SOOOO – SOOOO – SOOOO – SOOOO;

LISTEN NOW, HOW FAIR IT RINGS:

    SOOOO – SOOOO – SOOOO – SOOOO!

NOW ALL ARE RUNNING SWIFTLY HOME!

SH – SH – SHSH -- RUSHEL-WIND!

P'HHH – P'HHH -- BLOWING-WIND!

TI – TA – TOUSLE -- BLUSTER-WIND!

WHEE – WHEE – RRRRRR -- WHIRLY-WIND!

REMAINS THE SWAYING-WIND SO MILD,

HE SINGS A SONG FOR MY DEAR CHILD:

CD track 23

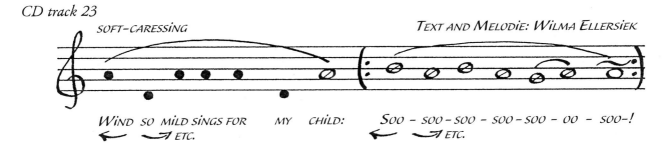

SOFT-CARESSING   TEXT AND MELODIE: WILMA ELLERSIEK

WIND SO MILD SINGS FOR   MY   CHILD: SOO – SOO – SOO – SOO – SOO – OO – SOO–!

←   ↗ ETC.   ←   ↗ ETC.

IN SLEEP MY CHILD LIES,

AND HOME THE WIND FLIES.

TEXT:

1   The wind sends his
                children about.
     From the wind house they
                come out.

HAND GESTURES:

1   For this game, it would be best to sit on a stool so that your arms can swing back freely. The whole upper body does the movement for the first two lines. Sit upright, extending your arms in front of you as if holding a large tray on your lower arms. Your fingers are loosely closed and lightly curled up. From this position, swing your upper body forward, almost down to your thighs, without moving your arms, just letting them swing along passively. To accompany this movement, speak: "The wind, he sends his..." At the moment when your upper body bounces back, your arms move backward a little more. Then, with a bound, your arms swing forward from underneath. This causes your upper body to dip down very low again, and then, together with your arms, swing back to the original position. The text to this movement is: "children about." Repeat the entire movement for the second line of text with the following break: "From the wind house," with the movement swinging down and back. Then for "they come out," your body swings back to its original

Note: The game can also be ended after 25, "In sleep my child lies." For older children, a good addition is the wind game with the ribbon wands on page 48.

Important note:

This wind game is organized as a rondo. In between a repetitive refrain, a story is told of different kinds of wind. It has a wonderful, musical construction. It begins with a soft wind, only rustling in the leaves. The Blowing-Wind, also, belongs rather to the more quiet winds. But the storm sweeps the land and even increases to a Whirly-Wind, but then slows down again to leave only a whisper.

The refrain should be spoken according to the wind that follows — in the beginning, therefore, slowly and quite softly. The listening to the wind is also a quiet gesture. For the Bluster-Wind and the Whirly-Wind the refrain also is spoken lively and loudly, and the listening lasts for a shorter time; for a loud wind, it is heard immediately. For the Swaying-Wind the voice volume decreases again. Speaking is slower and the speech melody closer to singing. Of course, intensive listening is needed to hear the soft Swaying-Wind.

Speech in this game is based strongly on the imitation of sound and therefore presupposes that the adult speaker articulates well. The play offers chil-

38

2   Listen here, can you tell me
      What this wind child's
               name might be?

3   SH – SH – shshsh,
      SH – SH – shshsh?

position. This movement is an uninterrupted swinging movement, no movement break must occur between swings. Practice first without speech until your body is familiar with the swinging.

2   Hold your right hand to your right ear while your upper body and head lightly lean to the front right, then speak: "Listen here…" At the word "you," which is slightly accented, your right hand with closed fingers, loosely stretched, and palms down, points at an imaginary place ahead at about chest height.

3   To give the "SH" more sound, speak it with pursed lips. Capital letters denote a loud wind sound, the small letters a soft sound. Lift your right lower arm and hand vertically, about face height, with your palm toward the children, your fingers loosely open and slightly stretched. A very fast, right-left turning originates from your lower arm, so that the fingers of your right hand look as if the wind shakes the leaves. For the loud "SH," your hand with its flitting fingers moves a little toward the children; for the softer "sh," your hand remains close to your face with weaker flit-

dren a holistic, optimal approach to strengthen and develop their speech through a connection of musically formed speech with imaginatively pictured nature experiences and phenomenologically fitting movements.

The leader should therefore allow the sound "sh" in the words "Rushel-wind," "rushels" and "shrubs" to sound a little longer than in "normal" speech. For the Blowing-Wind the sounds "b," "v" and "f" must be clearly articulated: "Blowing-Wind, blows, leaves, from." The Bluster-Wind excels through the sounds "st," "t" and "s:" "Bluster-Wind comes, ti – ta – tousles, soaring." With the voiceless "s," the storms whistling can literally be heard. Then follows the "wh" and "r." If possible, "r" should be rolled with the tongue: "Whirly-Wind, whirls, turns." With the Swaying-Wind, the ringing sounds must be emphasized as in the voiced "w" and "ng:" "Swaying, sings, song."

In this way the children are offered the possibility to form their speech without being made conscious of it. Never correct the children; practice comes through game repetition.

4 The Rushel-Wind rushels
                 the shrubs:
SH – SH – shshsh,
First loud: SH – SH,
Then soft: shshsh,
So sounds the Rushel-
                 Wind song:
SH – SH – shshsh!

5 The wind sends his
                 children about.
From the wind house they
                 come out.
Listen here, can you
                 tell me
What this wind child's
                 name might be?

6 P'hhh – p'hhh –
                 p'hhh – p'hhh?

7 The Blowing-Wind blows
     the leaves from the tree:
P'hhh – p'hhh –
                 p'hhh – p'hhh;

---

ting. Stop after the last
"shshsh" and look questioningly at the children.

4 Your right hand moves as
described in 3 each time
the sound "SH" occurs.
Continue with the differ-
entiation of loud "SH" and
soft "shshsh," by making
large, very fast, and then
small, slower movements.

5 As in 1.

6 With your fingers and
thumb tightly closed, and
with pointers touching the
sides of your nose, make a
megaphone around your
mouth with your hands.
For each "p'hhh," blow
gently while your upper
body moves a little toward
the children; simultaneous-
ly, slightly increase the
rounding of your hands.
Take a new breath for each
"p'hhh," then decrease the
movement again. The ges-
ture is a light pulsation.
After a short time, stop the
movement and blowing
and look at the children
questioningly.

7 Again, do the pulsating
movement as in 6 at each
word starting with a "B"
and at each "p'hhh."

8 And a beautiful dream he
blows for me:

P'hhh – p'hhh –
p'hhh – p'hhh.

9 The wind sends his
children about.
From the wind house they
come out.
Listen here, could you
tell me
What this wind child's
name might be?

10 Ti – ta – tousle,

Ti – ta – tousle?

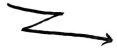

11 The Bluster-Wind
comes roaring:
He ti – ta – tousles!
He ti – ta – tousles!

8 Lift your hands above
your head as shown, then
move them down sideways
to describe a beautiful circle. Arrange the tempo of
the movement so that at
the word "dream," both
hands lie on your thighs,
palms up.

9 As in 1.

10 Lift your right arm and
hand with stretched,
closed fingers above your
head to the left side, so
that your arm covers your
face for a moment. From
there, your right arm cuts
an energetic "Z" through
the air, each syllable in its
own movement direction
(see left). Do this twice.

11 Now, lift your right hand
with stretched, closed fingers straight above your
head and let it circle vehe-
mently above your head

several times until the end of the line: "The Bluster-Wind comes roaring." At "he," move your right hand to the beginning of the Z position as in 10, and at "ti – ta – tousles," write the Z into the air.

12 And off again soaring!

12 After the last Z, quickly move your right hand in front of your belly, bending your wrist and elbow sharply, palm to the right and thumb pointing down. Quickly spread all your fingers before you move your arm behind your back in a fast, very lively movement. At the same time, form a fist as if to grab the wind.

13 The wind sends his
　　　　children about.
From the wind house they
　　　　come out.
Listen here, could you
　　　　tell me
What this wind child's
　　　　name might be?

13 As in 1.

14 Whee – whee – rrrrrr –
　　Whee – whee – rrrrrr?

14 Lay your left lower arm across both thighs, close to your knees, as a support for your upper body. Your right hand, with closed, loosely bent fingers, fingertips hanging down, draws a circle in the air before your knees. This circle can be pictured as lying horizontally before your knees. Its radius is as large as possible. With each "whee," describe a large circle. At "rrrrrr," decrease the circle

with a spiral movement
inward until your lower
arm has reached the center
and only your hand still
circles fast, very loosely
from your wrist.

15 The Whirly-Wind,
      he whirls around:
Whee – whee –
      whirl about;
Whee – whee – a
      whirling blast;
Whee – whee – turns
      so fast!

15 Retain the position as in
14. At "Whirly" and
"Wind" make a large circle
in front of your knees. At
"he whirls," decrease in a
spiral, and at "around,"
your hand circles alone.
Then, make a large circle at
each "whee," and a decreas-
ing spiral with your hand,
circling in the center for the
words following the "whee."

16 The wind sends his
      children about.
From the wind house they
      come out.
Listen here, can you
      tell me
What this wind child's
      name might be?

16 As in 1.

17 Soooo – soooo –

Soooo – soooo?

17 Hold your right hand
palm up, like a small bowl,
with closed, lightly bent
fingers at about the height
of your navel. Gently
swing to the left and right,
your upper body lightly
following. Change direc-
tion at each "soooo."

18 The Swaying-Wind,

he soughs and sings:

Soooo – soooo –

soooo – soooo;

18 Continue the movement
of 17, and rock according
to the movement arrows.

Listen now,

⌣ ⌣

    how fair it rings:

    ⌣ ⌣

Soooo – soooo –

⌣ ⌣

    soooo – soooo!

    ⌣ ⌣

19 Now all are running
    swiftly home!

19 Look at the children.

20 SH – SH – shsh --
    Rushel-Wind!

20 At the sound "SH," move
as described in 3, paying
attention to the change of
loud and soft. At "Rushel-
Wind," move your right
hand behind you in a
quiet movement.

21 P'hhh – p'hhh --
    Blowing-Wind!

21 Repeat the gesture for
"p'hhh," as in 6, and at
"Blowing-Wind," move both
hands behind your back.

22 Ti – ta – tousle --
    Bluster-Wind!

22 For "ti – ta – tousle," move
in a "Z," as in 10. At
"Bluster-Wind," move
your right hand quickly
behind as in 12.

23 Whee – whee – rrrrrr --
    Whirly-Wind!

23 Do the "whee – whee –
rrrrr" as in 14, and at
"Whirly-Wind," make
your right hand disappear
with the same intensity as
for the "Bluster-Wind."

24 Remains the Swaying

⌣ ⌣

    Wind so mild,

    ⌣ ⌣

He sings a song

⌣ ⌣

    for my dear child:

    ⌣ ⌣

24 Start singing: *Wind so
Mild Sings for My Child*,
p37, while making the soft
rocking movements as in
17. The change of direc-
tion for the rocking is
denoted with arrows under
the song text.

25 In sleep my child lies,

25 Rest your left cheek on your joined hands.

26 And home the wind flies.

26 From the "rest position," your right hand disappears behind your back in a quiet movement. The following hand

CD track 24

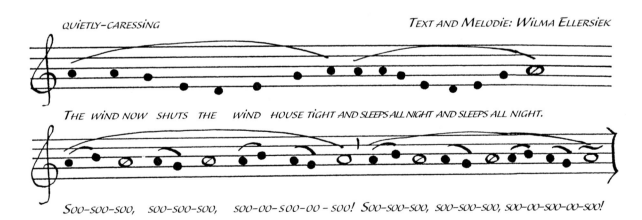

QUIETLY-CARESSING

TEXT AND MELODIE: WILMA ELLERSIEK

THE WIND NOW SHUTS THE WIND HOUSE TIGHT AND SLEEPS ALL NIGHT AND SLEEPS ALL NIGHT.

Soo-soo-soo, soo-soo-soo, soo-oo-soo-oo-soo! Soo-soo-soo, soo-soo-soo, soo-oo-soo-oo-soo!

27 The wind now shuts the **wind house tight**

gestures accompany the song text:

27 Spread your arms to the right and left and close them slowly in a circle in front of you. At the word "tight," your hands move in front of each other.

45

28 and sleeps all night
       and sleeps all night

28 Join your hands, move
     them to the left, and rest
     your head on them.

29 Soo – soo – soo,

    Soo – soo – soo,

    Soo – oo – soo – oo – soo! –

    Soo – soo – soooo,

    Soo – soo – soooo,

    Soo – oo – soo – oo – soo! –

29 In the position of 28, gen-
     tly rock according to the
     arrows. At the last "soooo,"
     lift your head, and with
     your hands above your
     head make a circle down
     your sides and to your
     thighs. At the end, lay
     your hands flat on your
     thighs and remain sitting a
     little while, letting the
     game resonate.

Ribbon Wand, Magic Wand

Sound Gesture Game with Sound Producing Instruments

RIBBON WAND, MAGIC WAND, CALL FORTH FOR ME A WIND.
   CALL FORTH FOR ME A SHSHSHSH – RUSHEL-WIND.
   SH – SH – SHSHSH, SH – SH – SHSHSH.
   SH – SH – SHSHSH, SH – SH – SHSHSH.

RIBBON WAND, MAGIC WAND, CALL FORTH FOR ME A WIND.
   CALL FORTH FOR ME A P'HHHHHHH – BLOWING-WIND.
   P'HHHH – P'HHHH – P'HHHHHHH.
   P'HHHH – P'HHHH – P'HHHHHHH.

RIBBON WAND, MAGIC WAND, CALL FORTH FOR ME A WIND.
   CALL FORTH FOR ME A SSSSSSSST – BLUSTER-WIND.
   SSSST – SSSSST – SSSSSSST.
   SSSST – SSSSST – SSSSSSST.

RIBBON WAND, MAGIC WAND, CALL FORTH FOR ME A WIND.
   CALL FORTH FOR ME A WHEE-WHEE – WHIRLY-WIND.
   WHEE – WHEE – WHEEEE.
   DRRRRR – DRRRRR.

RIBBON WAND, MAGIC WAND, CALL FORTH FOR ME A WIND.
   CALL FORTH FOR ME A SSSSSSOOOO – WHISPER-WIND.
   SSSSSS – SSSSSS – SSSSSSOOOO.
   SSSSSS – SSSSSS – SSSSSSOOOO.

TEXT:	WAND MOVEMENTS:

TEXT:

1 Ribbon Wand,

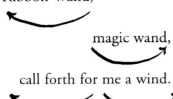

        magic wand,

  call forth for me a wind.

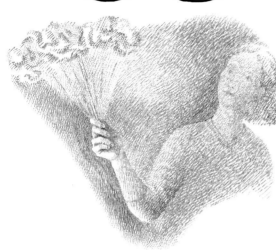

Call forth for me a
Shshshsh – Rushel-wind.
~~~~~~~~~~~~~~~~

SH – SH – shshsh,
~~~~~ ~~~~~

SH – SH – shshsh.
~~~~~ ~~~~~

SH – SH – shshsh,
~~~~~ ~~~~~

SH – SH – shshsh.
~~~~~ ~~~~~

2 Ribbon Wand, magic

     wand, call forth for

        me a wind.

Call forth for me a
P'hhhhhhh – Blowing-wind.
P'hhhh – P'hhhh –
         P'hhhhhhh.
P'hhhh – P'hhhh –
         P'hhhhhhh.

WAND MOVEMENTS:

1 Hold the ribbon wand vertically in front of you, so that the ribbons are about face height. Look kindly at your wand as you swing it lightly to and fro in the given rhythm. Then shake the wand at each "Sh." However, do not speak the first "sh." Starting with "Rushel-wind," speak all the sounds. At "SH," speak the sound forcefully and shake the wand energetically; at "sh," speak softly and shake gently. Speech must be rhythmical and sound oriented.

2 First line as in 1. Now hold the wand horizontally, so that the ribbons hang down and the point of the wand is before your mouth. For each "P'hhhh" blow lightly against the ribbons.

Craft directions for making a ribbon wand are offered on page 142.

3 Ribbon Wand,

magic wand, call forth

for me a wind.

Call forth for me a
Sssssssst – Bluster-wind.

Sssst – sssssst – sssssssst.

Sssst – sssssst – sssssssst.

4 Ribbon Wand,

magic wand, call forth

for me a wind.

Call forth for me a
whee-whee – Whirly-wind.

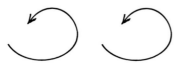

3   First line as in 1. For the first "Sssssssst," which is not sounded out loud, make an energetic "Z" into the air with the wand, and for each additional "sssst," beat the ribbon wand strongly up and down. Direct this movement with only the lower arm, as it may get too large otherwise.

4   First line as in 1. Now lift up the ribbon wand and starting with "whee," move strongly in circles with it, above your head. Don't sound the first "whee."

Whee – whee – wheeee.

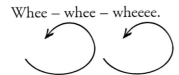

Drrrrr – drrrrr.

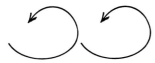

5   Ribbon Wand,

magic wand, call forth

for me a wind.

Call forth for me a
Sssssso0o0o – Whisper-wind.

Sssss – sssss – Ssssss0o0o.

Sssss – sssss – Ssssss0o0o.

5   First line as in 1. Then
hold the ribbon wand hor-
izontally before you so that
the ribbons hang freely
before your knees.
Without voicing the first
"sssso0o0," start a gentle
swaying motion with the
upper body. The arrows
show the change of direc-
tion. Instead of "Whisper-
wind," one can say
"Swaying-wind." Speak the
"ssss," voiced. At the end
of the text, continue
swinging the ribbon wand;
after a short silence, begin
to sing, continuing with
the swaying movement
until the end of the song.

The Wind He Comes Along

CD track 25

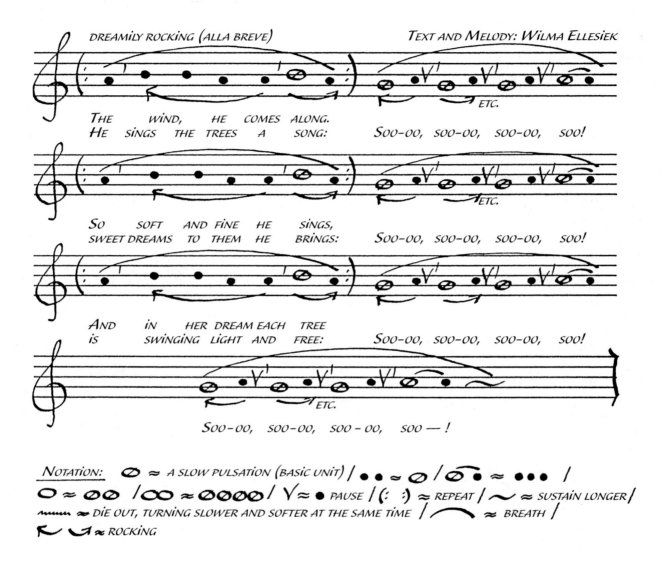

DREAMILY ROCKING (ALLA BREVE)

TEXT AND MELODY: WILMA ELLESIEK

THE WIND, HE COMES ALONG.
HE SINGS THE TREES A SONG: Soo-oo, soo-oo, soo-oo, soo!

SO SOFT AND FINE HE SINGS,
SWEET DREAMS TO THEM HE BRINGS: Soo-oo, soo-oo, soo-oo, soo!

AND IN HER DREAM EACH TREE
IS SWINGING LIGHT AND FREE: Soo-oo, soo-oo, soo-oo, soo!

Soo-oo, soo-oo, soo-oo, soo — !

NOTATION: ⊘ ≈ A SLOW PULSATION (BASIC UNIT) / ● ● ≈ ⊘ / ⊘ ● ≈ ● ● ● /
○ ≈ ⊘⊘ / ○○ ≈ ⊘⊘⊘⊘ / V ≈ ● PAUSE / (: :) ≈ REPEAT / ~ ≈ SUSTAIN LONGER /
∿∿∿ ≈ DIE OUT, TURNING SLOWER AND SOFTER AT THE SAME TIME / ⌒ ≈ BREATH /
↶ ↷ ≈ ROCKING

Following the song, rest the ribbon wand in your lap and stroke once, gently, across the ribbons.

Autumn Wind

THE AUTUMN WIND COMES:
WHEE – WHEE! HOH – HO-O-OH!
FROM THE BRANCH:
RICKETY – WRENCH, RICKETY – WRENCH!
THE LEAVES HE DOES TEAR.
THEY'RE FLYING, FLYING THROUGH THE AIR.
WHIRLING – WHIRLING.
ROCKING – ROCKING.
HOVERING – HOVERING.
TURNING – TURNING.
SINKING SO GENTLY DOWN TO THE EARTH,
REMAIN LYING,
DREAMING OF FLYING.

THE AUTUMN WIND, HE RUNS AND LEAPS,
BLOWS: FFFF! IN THE LEAVES' BIG HEAPS:
SH – SH – SHATTER – SHATTER,
WHISPER AND CHATTER.
SH – SH – SHATTER – SHATTER
SH – SH – SH – SH.
THEN HE RUNS OFF: FFFF – FFFFFF.
UNDER THE BARE TREES, DEEP,
AUTUMN LEAVES LIE, IN DREAM, AND SLEEP.

TEXT:		HAND GESTURES:	
1	The autumn wind comes:	1	Look brightly at the children and call with a light, happy voice: "The autumn wind comes."
2	Whee – whee!	2	For the first syllable, "whee," your arms and hands (fingers stretched and closed) make a lively movement from high on the right to about chest height. Then, make a small

Before continuing with 15, the game may be amended in the following way:

Ask the children: "Of what else do the leaves dream?" and then silently show, for example, the turning of the leaves. (Directions for turning, are in 11.) The children imitate the movement. Again, ask and then show one of the "leaf-movements;" or ask one child: "Of

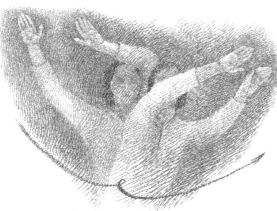

loop backwards to get a new impetus; with the second "whee," swing up to the left. Sound the "wh" and "ee" as resonantly as possible.

3 Hoh – ho-o-oh!

3 Put your closed hands (thumbs lie tightly next to pointers) as a megaphone to your mouth, so that your pointers lie alongside your nose. Strongly sound the "oh."

4 From the branch:

4 Stretch both arms sideways and up, with spread fingers, as a tree with branches.

5 Rickety – wrench,
        rickety – wrench!

5 Shake your hands heartily, with the movement originating from your wrist. Your fingers must be very relaxed.

6 The leaves he does tear.

6 Your arms remain raised up and at the words "leaves" and "tear" strongly throw your hands up.

what do your leaves dream?"

When the child shows a leaf-movement, immediately play along, encouraging the other children to imitate also.

Don't continue this play for too long, but at the right moment continue with 15.

The next two games, *In the Fir Wood* and *By the Oak Tree* are extension games to the *Autumn Wind.* One could characterize these two games as extended hand gesture games, for they are particularly suitable to be played kneeling on the floor. In *In the Fir Wood,* the upper part of the body also participates with the movements and therefore could be called a "large gesture movement game."

When the autumn wind is your seasonal theme, both supplementary games can be played independently, as they are each complete in themselves. It is also possible to add only one of the extension games to the primary game. Since the autumn theme will be in use over several weeks it might also be fun to add the other two to the primary game, step by step.

The lullaby: *The Wind Now Shuts the Wind House Tight* on page 67 could also be used already in the game *In the Fir Wood.* Then, only sing the first verse. If this makes the song too short, hum the second verse.

7   They're flying,
         flying through the air.

8   Whirling – whirling.

9   Rocking – rocking.

10 Hovering – hovering.

11 Turning – turning.

7   Dissolve the tree gesture and bring your hands, palms down, together in front of your forehead as "leaves" floating lightly up and down. Speech must be very melodious.

8   Take your hands down to stomach height, with the back of your hands toward the children, turning them quickly around each other. If possible, accentuate and roll the "r" as in "whirrrrrling."

9   In the previous position, turn your hands so that your palms are up, with your fingers together and slightly bent, like a bowl. As shown with arrows, your hands swing together, right and left. Speak each syllable at various tone heights.

10 Return your hands to the same position as in 7. For "hovering," your hands remain at the same height, but are very calmly moved right and left. Your voice, too, remains at the same pitch, the "o" in "ho-o-overing" stretched out or somewhat sung.

11 Move your hands down again; lower arms are held horizontally, with hands hanging down, so that the backs of your hands face

each other, fingertips pointing downward. In this position, turn your hands lightly at the wrist.

12 Sinking so gently down
        to the earth,

12 Start again with your hands in position 7. Now, let them sink down with a gentle twirling. At "earth," arrive with your hands on your knees or the floor. Your voice, also, should sink with your hands. Turn over one or both hands after they have touched the earth like a wilted leaf. For a while, let the leaves lie on the ground, while looking at them.

13 Remain lying,

13 Stretch out the "y" in the word "lying," your voice level, not sinking at the end of the word. Nod your head in confirmation. Then make a small pause.

14 Dreaming of flying.

14 Sing the word "dreaming," softly and gently on one pitch; make a small pause, then speak the words "of flying" in a very high voice, almost singing. Then, silently repeat the movements as described in 7 and 12.

A – E Extention game. See page 58.

15 The autumn wind,

15 Look again at the children and call out in a bright, joyful voice: "The autumn wind."

16 he runs and leaps,

16 Movement as in 2.

17 Blows: Ffff!

17 Make a megaphone as in 3 and blow strongly: "Ffff!"

18 In the leaves' big heaps:

19 Sh – sh – shatter – shatter,
    Whisper and chatter.
    Sh – sh – shatter – shatter,
    Sh – sh – sh – sh.

20 Then he runs off:

21 Ffff – ffffff.
22 Under the bare trees, deep,

23 Autumn leaves lie,

24 In dream, and sleep.

18 With both hands, show a
    large, imaginary leaf pile.
19 Hold your hands, palms
    down, at about stomach
    height, turning them in
    and out very fast, so that a
    whirring movement results.
    One moves around in the
    leaf pile so that a chatter-
    ing noise results. Speak the
    "sh" with pursed lips to
    create a good sound.

20 Look brightly at the chil-
    dren and call out with a
    strong-sounding voice:
    "then he runs off."

21 As in 17.
22 Hold your arms up as in
    4, with spread fingers.
    Allow plenty of time to
    show the bare branches to
    the children.

23 Slowly move your hands
    down, as in 12.

24 Nod your head for
    "dream," pause, then add:
    "and sleep" in a dark voice.

Extension Game

A   Sing the song *Autumn Leaves Dream of Flying*

Autumn Leaves Dream of Flying

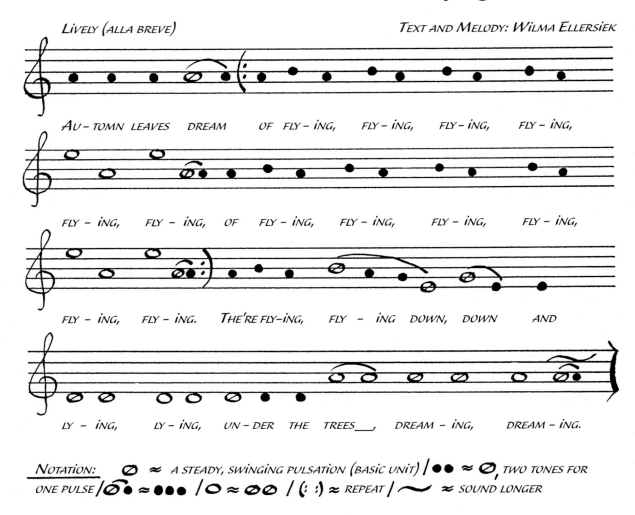

B   Sing the song *Autumn Leaves Dream*.
Ask the children: "Of what [else] do the
leaves dream?" and then silently show, for
example, the turning of the leaves.
(Directions for turning are in 11.)
The children imitate the movement.

Autumn Leaves Dream

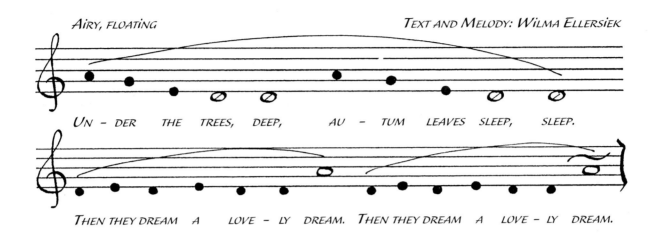

C   Repeat the song *Autumn Leaves Dream*.
Again, ask and then show one of the "leaf-
movements;" or ask one child: "Of what do
your leaves dream?" When the child shows a
leaf-movement, immediately play along,
encouraging the other children to imitate also.

D   Repeat the song *Autumn Leaves Dream* and
repeat questions etc.

E   End question games with the song: *Leaves
Are so Tired*. Don't continue this play for
too long, but at the right moment continue
with 15.

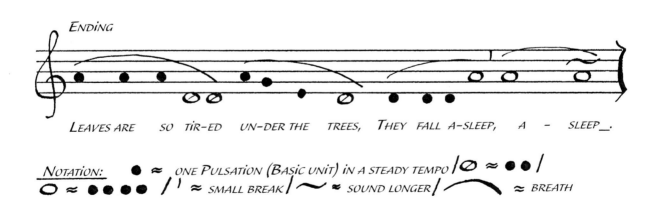

Autumn Wind in the Fir Wood

WHEE – HOH – HO-O-OH!
WHEE – HOH – HO-O-OH!

THE AUTUMN WIND COMES RUNNING ALONG:
RUNS – RUNS – RUNS – RUNS.
WHEE – HOH - HO-O-OH!
WHEE – HOH – HO-O-OH!

HE COMES TO THE FIR WOOD STRONG:
BENDS – BENDS – BENDS – DOWN
THE TALL FIR'S CROWN.

CONES TUMBLE:
BUB – BOB – POP – THEY DROP,
BUB – BOB – POP – THEY DROP,
BUB – BOB – POP!
THEY LIE ALL – GREAT AND SMALL –
QUIET ON THE MOSSY GROUND – WITHOUT A SOUND!

TEXT:

1 Whee – hoh – ho-o-oh!
   Whee – hoh – ho-o-oh!

2 The autumn wind comes
      running along:

GESTURES:

1 For this game, it is particularly suitable to play on the floor, kneeling down. But it can also be played sitting on a stool or chair. First make a megaphone with both hands without touching your mouth directly with your hands. Call strongly: "Whee."

2 Gathering force from behind, throw both arms forward in a strong movement. Your arms are relaxed, your hands open, and your fingers lightly stretched and closed. Leave air between your

3   Runs – runs – runs – runs.

4   Whee – hoh - ho-o-oh!
     Whee – hoh – ho-o-oh!

5   He comes to the fir
                wood strong:

6   Bends – bends –
     ← ——→

                bends – down
                ← ——→

7   The tall fir's crown.
     ← ——→

8   Cones tumble: —

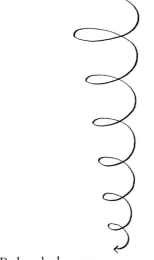

9   Bub – bob – pop –
     •   •   •

                they drop,
                     •

body and your arms. Your upper body moves along with your arm movement.

3   **Swing** both hands from right to left in four large arcs. Stretch the word "run" each time, almost calling. Now, briefly pause in order to be ready for the slower movement.

4   As in 1.

5   Stretch your arms high above your head, palms joined with closed fingers as the "fir's crown."

6   The fir's crown bends. Slowly bend your upper body from your waist to the right and left in a "fir tree" position.

7   As in 6.

8   Dissolve the fir tree position, but make fists with your hands above your head. At the word "tumble," quickly turn your fists – as cones – about each other, while moving your arms down to your knees or the floor. Strongly sound the "m" in tumble.

9   Let your right and left fists, as "fir cones," bounce on your thighs or the floor. For the last "pop," bounce

Bub – bob – pop –
•   •   •
           they drop,
                •
Bub – bob – pop!
•   •   •

10 They lie all – great
                and small –

11 Quiet

12 On the mossy ground –
     without a sound.

both fists at the same time, slowing down the speed. 9 can be repeated.

10 Very peacefully say: "They lie all," while looking at your fists lying quietly on your thighs or the floor. When saying "great," join your fists together and show this to the children. Then, for "small," separate your fists and show each one individually.

11 Return your fists to your thighs or the floor and hold them quietly.

12 At "mossy," open your fists; slowly and gently stroke your flat palms over your thighs or the floor. Slowly and pleasurably speak the word "mossy;" at the word "ground," delicately rest your hands on the "moss." Hold this gesture for a while, and so end the game.

Autumn Wind by the Oak Tree

ALL IS STILL! – THE WIND RAN ON –
TO ANOTHER PLACE HAS GONE!
WHEE – HOH – HO-O-OH!
WHEE – HOH – HO-O-OH!
THE WIND RUNS AND RUNS AND RUNS.
WHEE – HOH – HO-O-OH!
WHEE – HOH – HO-O-OH!
HE COMES TO THE OAK TREE, TALL AND BROAD.

SWEEPS – SWEEPS – SWEEPS THROUGH THE CROWN,
SHAKES THE BRANCHES UP AND DOWN – UP AND DOWN.
THE ACORNS FALL:
TECK – TECK – TECKA – TECK!
TECK – TECK – TECKA – TECK!
THEY JUMP AND CRACK:
POCK – POCK – PECKA – PACK!
POCK – POCK – PECKA – PACK!
POCK! – POCK! – PACK!
THEN LIE QUIET – THE WHOLE LOT –
VERY QUIET IN ONE SPOT.

ALL IS STILL! – THE WIND RAN ON –
WHEE – HOH – HO-O-OH!
WHEE – HOH – HO-O-OH!
HE RUNS – RUNS – RUNS HOME.
HE SHUTS THE WIND HOUSE TIGHT,
AND RESTS AT NIGHT.

TEXT:	GESTURES:
1 All is still! – 	1 Put your hands behind your ears and listen quietly. Then begin speaking the line.

2 The wind ran on – to
   another place has gone!

2 Lift your hands. At "on," and "another," move them in an arc forward, pointing toward the distance.

3 Whee – hoh – ho-o-oh!
   Whee – hoh – ho-o-oh!

3 Form a megaphone with your hands, without them touching your mouth, and call: "Whee."

4 The wind runs and runs
   and runs.

4 Swing both hands from right to left in four large arcs. Slowly speak the word "run," almost as a call.

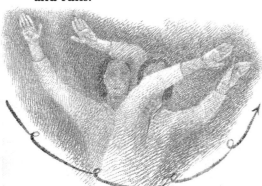

5 Whee – hoh – ho-o-oh!
   Whee – hoh – ho-o-oh!

5 As in 3.

6 He comes to the oak tree,
   tall and broad.

6 Raise your arms and hands, holding them parallel until they are stretched, creating a tall tree. At "broad," spread your arms and hands, with stretched fingers, as the tree's branches and twigs. Allow plenty of time for speech and movement.

7 Sweeps – sweeps – sweeps

   through the crown,

7 Move your arms and hands in lively swings from right to left. At "crown," stretch your arms and hands, with spread fingers, a little forward, palms down.

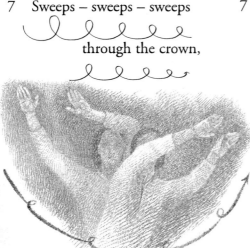

8   Shakes the branches

↓ ↓   ↑ ↑
  r /   r /

up and down –

↓   ↓
  r   /

up and down.

↑   ↑
  r   /

9   The acorns fall:
    Teck – teck – tecka – teck!
    Teck – teck – tecka – teck!

10 They jump and crack:

11 Pock – pock –
                  pecka – pack!
    Pock – pock –
                  pecka – pack!
12 Pock! – Pock! – Pack!

13 Then lie quiet – the whole
                  lot – Very quiet in

8   Shake your hands up and
    down in a strong and
    lively way from the wrist
    as shown by the arrows.
    You may shake them
    more often, or repeat 8.

9   Raise your fists, the bent
    pointers protruding as
    "acorns." At "fall," quick-
    ly move your hands
    down, so that you can
    drum "teck – teck – teck"
    on your thighs or the
    floor in a free rhythm.

10 For "jump," and "crack,"
    knock with your pointer
    knuckles together on your
    thighs or the floor,
    bouncing off again.

11 As described above at 9,
    rhythmically drum with
    the acorns on your thighs
    or the floor.

12 At "pock – pock – pack,"
    knock with bent pointers
    together, letting them
    bounce back.

13 Rest your bent pointers
    on your thighs or on
    the floor and keep
    them quiet.

14 one spot.

14 Turn your hands and
   show the "spot" with
   your pointers.

15 All is still! –
        The wind ran on –
16 Whee – hoh – ho-o-oh!
   Whee – hoh – ho-o-oh!
   He runs – runs – runs
17 home.

15 As in 1 and 2.

16 As in 3 and 4.

17 Swing your hands in an
   arc from front to back
   while separating them to
   both sides of your body.

18 He shuts the wind
              house tight,

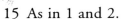

18 Now, bring your hands
   together in a wide arc,
   wrapping them around
   each other. Slowly speak
   the word "tight."

19 And rests at night.

19 Speak slowly, in a dark
   voice; at "night," nod
   your head once.

The Wind Now Shuts the Wind House Tight

CD track 24

QUIETLY-CARESSING

TEXT AND MELODY: WILMA ELLERSIEK

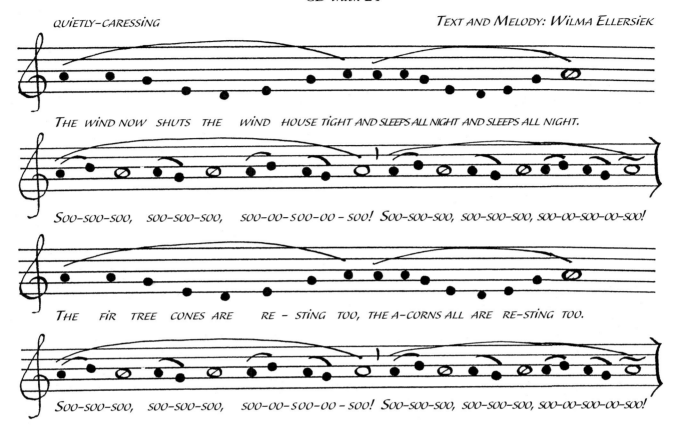

The wind now shuts the wind house tight and sleeps all night and sleeps all night.

Soo-soo-soo, soo-soo-soo, soo-oo-soo-oo-soo! Soo-soo-soo, soo-soo-soo, soo-oo-soo-oo-soo!

The fir tree cones are re-sting too, the a-corns all are re-sting too.

Soo-soo-soo, soo-soo-soo, soo-oo-soo-oo-soo! Soo-soo-soo, soo-soo-soo, soo-oo-soo-oo-soo!

Halloween Song
CD track 26

HAPPY AND LIVELY   *TEXT AND MELODY: WILMA ELLERSIEK*

WE'RE PLAY – iNG   HAL-LOW-EEN TO   DAY,   SHiMM – SHiMM––––SHAW!
COME, LiT – TLE   FOLK, AND   PLAY____: SHiMM – SHiMM–––SHAW!

HEE – HA – HEE – HA – HALLOW – EEN: TiMM – – TOOM – – TAW!
iT'S WAL – LOW––WEEN   TO – DAY!   TiMM – – TOOM – – TAW!

THiS iS DONE, THAT   iS DONE,   WE   MAKE   FUN,   WE   MAKE   FUN:
THiS iS DONE, THAT   iS DONE,   WE   MAKE   FUN,   WE   MAKE   FUN:

PiMM – MA – PUMM–––MA – – PAY   ON HAL – LOW – EEN – DAY____.
PiMM – MA – PUMM–––MA – – PAY   ON HAL – LOW – EEN – DAY____.

NOTATION: ● ≈ ONE PULSATION (BASiC UNiT) iN MiDDLE TEMPO | ⊘ ≈ ●● |
O ≈ ●●●● / (: :) ≈ REPEAT / ~ SUSTAIN TONE LONGER

TEXT:

1 We're playing
        ↑
     Halloween today,
        ↑   ↑   ↑

2 Shim – shim – shaw –
     ～～～～

3 Hee – haw – hee – haw –
     ↑   ↑
              Halloween:
                 ↑   ↑

HAND GESTURES:

1 1 At ↑ beat jingle stick
   gently forward with your
   raised arm.

2 At ～～～ shake the
   jingle stick with your arm
   raised high.

3 As in 1.

INTRODUCTION:

It is highly recommended to
accompany this happy song
with jingle sticks. It is important that there is a jingle stick
available for each child. The
older kindergarten children
may perhaps help with crafting
the jingle sticks.

Craft directions for making
a jingle stick are offered on
page 143.

4 Tim – toom – taw –

〰〰〰

5 This is done, that is done,

     x ⌡   ⌡   *x* ⌡   ⌡

We have fun, we have fun,

     x ⌡   ⌡   *x* ⌡   ⌡

6 Pimma – pooma – pay

〰〰〰

7 On Halloween day.

    ↓   ↓

---

4 As in 2.

5 Tip the jingle stick with the jingles against your palm. The movement must be light and bouncy. Then move both hands in a small circle starting upwards. ⌡   ⌡

6 As in 2.

7 Beat with the end of the jingle stick against your left fist on the area where your pointer surrounds your thumb. Your left fist bounces back. Then, after the last beat lift up your jingle stick during a long, drawn-out note: "…day." Hold for a while. Repeat everything for the second verse.

PRELUDE:

Bring the jingle sticks covered in a basket. Shake the basket and let all listen to the sound until it has died down. Then shake the basket again. When all is quiet again, start with the verse:

i   The jingle sticks ring.

ii   And a song we will sing.

iii Now uncover the basket:

iv   I'll take one for each of you out,

v   And pass them about.

When everyone has a jingle stick, lift your own as high as your head and shake it with the words:

vi   Jingle stick: now shinga – shing,

vii Jingle stick: now binga – bing.

Wait until the sound of the jingles as abated, then start the Halloween Song. All can sing and play either in their seats or parading around the room.

POSTLUDE:

At the end of the song, say:

i   Pimma – pooma – pun –

ii   The song is done.

Now get the jingle stick basket:

iii The jingle sticks I'll gather all,

iv   We'll put them in the basket small.

After they are gathered, cover the basket with the colored cloth:

v   With this cloth I cover them tight,

vi In the basket they'll sleep all night.

Put away the covered basket.

Fog – Fog – Everywhere

I WOULD LIKE TO TAKE A WALK.
    THROUGH THE DOOR I STEP OUTSIDE.
    CANNOT SEE. OH NO!
    FOG – FOG – EVERYWHERE,
    SLOWLY I MUST GO.

CAREFULLY I MAKE MY WAY.
    GROPING – GROPING – GROPING – STAY...
    CANNOT SEE. OH NO!
    FOG – FOG – EVERYWHERE,
    SLOWLY I MUST GO.

CAREFULLY I MAKE MY WAY.
    GROPING – GROPING – GROPING – STAY...
    CANNOT SEE. OH NO!
    FOG – FOG – EVERYWHERE,
    SLOWLY I MUST GO.

CAREFULLY I MAKE MY WAY.
    GROPING – GROPING – STANDING STILL.
    WHERE DO I STAND NOW? — WHERE?
    HEY! – IT IS MY HOUSE! – BEFORE
    I CAME OUT OF THIS DOOR.
    WENT IN CIRCLES ROUND AND ROUND,
    IN FOG – IN FOG – IN FOG.

THROUGH THE DOOR I STEP INSIDE,
    WAIT UNTIL THE SUN SHINES BRIGHT.

TEXT:	HAND GESTURES:
1 I would like to take a walk.	1 At "I," point to yourself with both hands and at "walk," turn your hands forward to show where, outside, you want to walk.
2 Through the door · · r / I step outside. · · r /	2 Starting close to your body, "walk" on your thighs with flat hands alternating between the right and the left. Move toward your knees, up to the middle of your thighs. Start with the balls of your hands, rolling across your palms to your fingertips, imitating the movement of feet.
3 Cannot see. Oh no!	3 Touch your hands to your forehead and look searchingly about.
4 Fog – fog – everywhere, ← → →← r / r / r /	4 Hold your hands at chest height and "grope" in the fog, with your palms toward the children. As the arrows underneath the text on the left show, your hands move apart, then toward each other, then in an arc up and apart. Say the word "everywhere" slowly and in a stretched out manner.
5 Slowly I must go. · · r /	5 At "slowly," make a calming gesture towards the children. At the words "I must," slowly move your hands down to your left thigh and set them down like feet in two steps.
6 Carefully I make my way. · · · · r / r /	6 Continue walking with your hands on your left thigh toward your knee.

7 Groping – groping – groping –	7 Lift both hands and grope in the air with outstretched fingertips sideways to the left as if blind.
8 stay…	8 Let your arms and hands sink down to your body in a gesture that shows a moment of uncertainty, of waiting, of considering what to do.
9 Cannot see. Oh no! Fog – fog – everywhere, Slowly I must go.	9 Gestures as in 3, 4 and 5. As the text repeats itself in the following verses, so, accordingly, do the gestures.
10 Carefully I make my way.	10 The direction at "carefully I make my way" changes: midway to the front on both thighs (keep thighs together for this).
11 Groping — groping – groping – stay…	11 As in 7 and 8.
12 Cannot see. Oh no! Fog – fog – everywhere, Slowly I must go.	12 As in 3, 4 and 5
13 Carefully I make my way.	13 Walk with your hands to the right on your right thigh. Groping follows the same direction. Then the game continues.
14 Groping – groping, standing still.	14 With a small accent, put both flat hands down on your right thigh and pause for a short moment.
15 Where do I stand now?	15 Emphasize the word "**stand**," looking down at **your** hands that are still **resting** on your thighs.
16 Where? –	16 Look up, spreading **your** hands sideways **as in a** question.

17 Hey! – It is my house! –

17 During a small pause, show a look of surprise, for it is now clear where you stand. Then call "Hey!" Lift your hands up to about throat height and bring them together in a soft clap.

18 Before

18 Your arms and hands form a "roof" over your head with your stretched fingertips touching.

19 I came out of this door.

19 Dissolve the roof gesture, lower your hands and gesture with your fingertips toward your belly At "door," lay both flat hands down on your thighs.

20 Went in circles round

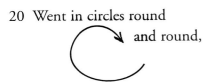

and round,

20 With both hands together, palms down, describe a large circle.

21 In fog – in fog – in fog.
22 Through the door I

step inside,

21 As in 3.
22 Again make a roof.

23 Wait until the sun shines bright.

23 Fold your arms and sit quietly for a while.

CD track 27

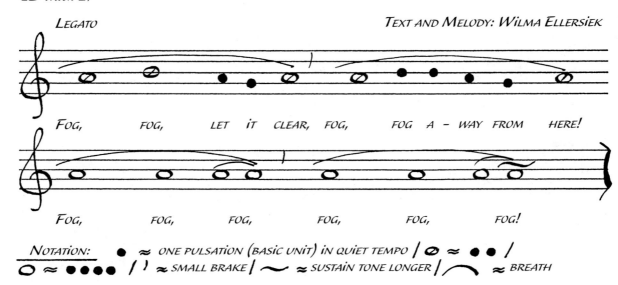

LEGATO   TEXT AND MELODY: WILMA ELLERSIEK

Fog,   Fog,   LET   IT   CLEAR,   Fog,   FOG   A – WAY FROM   HERE!

Fog,   Fog,   Fog,   Fog,   Fog,   Fog!

NOTATION: ● ≈ ONE PULSATION (BASIC UNIT) IN QUIET TEMPO | ⊘ ≈ ● ● |
⊘ ≈ ● ● ● ● | ⸍ ≈ SMALL BRAKE | ⁓ ≈ SUSTAIN TONE LONGER | ⌣ ≈ BREATH

a Fog, fog, let it clear,

b Fog, fog, away from here!

c Fog – fog – fog
   ⁓⁓⁓⁓⁓→
           Fog – fog
           ⁓⁓⁓→

d fog!

a Make a megaphone by cupping your hands around your mouth.

b Point with both hands far away, keeping them parallel with palms down.

c Make a horizontal, wavy line in the air with both hands. For the second line of the song, start again on the left and make the wavy line to the right.

d Show a large flat space with both hands, palms down. Start at the belly and move forward and sideways. Then pause.

My Bright Lantern
CD track 28

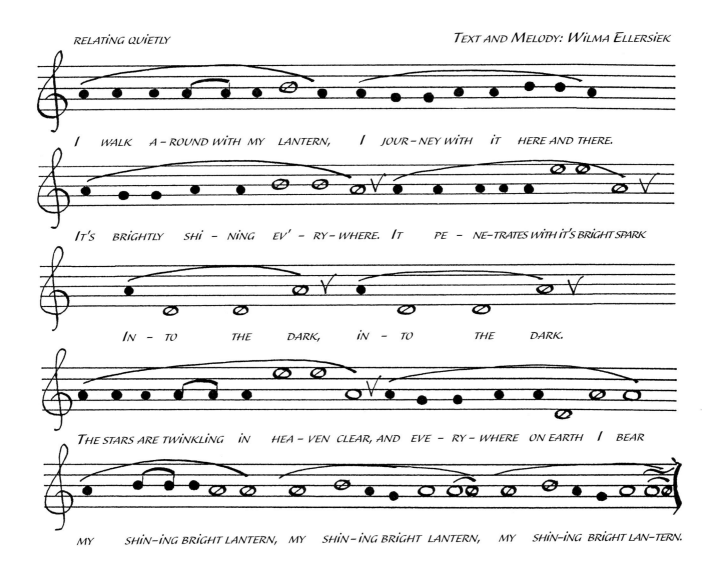

RELATING QUIETLY

TEXT AND MELODY: WILMA ELLERSIEK

I WALK A-ROUND WITH MY LANTERN, I JOUR-NEY WITH IT HERE AND THERE.

IT'S BRIGHTLY SHI-NING EV'-RY-WHERE. IT PE-NE-TRATES WITH IT'S BRIGHT SPARK

IN-TO THE DARK, IN-TO THE DARK.

THE STARS ARE TWINKLING IN HEA-VEN CLEAR, AND EVE-RY-WHERE ON EARTH I BEAR

MY SHIN-ING BRIGHT LANTERN, MY SHIN-ING BRIGHT LANTERN, MY SHIN-ING BRIGHT LAN-TERN.

NOTATION: ⊘ ≈ A SLOW PULSATION (BASIC UNIT) /●● ≈ ⊘ /♫ ≈ ● /
⌒○ ≈ ⊘⊘ /⌒○○ ≈ ⊘⊘⊘ /∨ ≈ PAUSE OF HALF A UNIT / ～ ≈ SUSTAIN LONGER /
⌢ ≈ BREATH

77

St. Nicholaus Song

CD track 29

Comfortable

Text and Melody: Wilma Ellersiek

St. Ni-cho-laus, St. Ni-cho-laus, he comes to-day to ev'ry house

with his great, big sack: pick-a-back, pick-a-back: he walks a long

stump, stump, stump, stump, stump, stump, stump, stump! The sack is full,

is hea-vy too: stump, stump, stump, stump, stump, stump, stump, stump

Ni-cho-laus, Ni-cho-laus! Please al-so come to ou-r house

with your great, big sack!_ And un-pack! – And un-pack!—

Notaion: ● ≈ one pulsation (basic unit) in a middle tempo | ⊘ ≈ ● ● |
○ ≈ ● ● ● ● | √ ≈ pause of one unit | √√ ≈ pause of two units |
∼ ≈ sustain longer

78

TEXT:

1   St. Nicholaus, St. Nicholaus,

2   He comes today to
        every house,

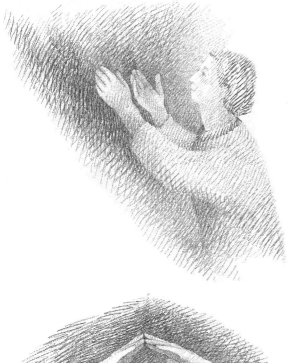

3   With his great, big sack.

4   *silent*

HAND GESTURES:

1   Turn to the children and
    nod as you sing the name:
    "Nicholaus."

2   At "comes," wave to your-
    self with both hands. For
    "house," show a roof over
    your head with your arms
    and hands.

3   Show the big, imaginary
    sack in front of you,
    from top to bottom,
    with both hands.

4   Rise from your seat and
    bend down to the right
    towards your sack.

Make movements in one of
the following positions:

A. sitting in a circle of chairs
    or stools;

B. standing in a circle;

C. standing freely in
    the room.

PRONUNCIATION:
Nicholaus rhymes with house.

Use this game in early
December in preparation for
St. Nicholaus Day on
December 6th, or as a prepara-
tion for the St. Nicholaus
Movement Game in a later
volume by Wilma Ellersiek.

79

5   Oof!

6   Picka – back –
                picka – back,

7   He walks along:
         r   /
    Stump – stump –
         r   /
               stump – stump –
                   r   /
    Stump – stump –
         r   /
               stump – stump!
                   r   /
    The sack is full,
       r   /   r /
    is heavy, too:
    r / r   /
    Stump – stump –
         r   /
               stump – stump –
                   r   /
    stump – stump –
               stump – stump!
      r   /   r   /

8   Aah!

9   Nicholaus! – Nicholaus!

---

5   Now grab the imaginary sack on the top with both hands and with "oof," swing it over your back, across your right shoulder, holding on tight with both hands.

6   At "picka-back," bounce a bit in your knees to show that the sack is heavy.

7   At "he walks," slowly shift your body weight to your left leg and start lifting your right leg. At "along," start walking slowly, bent over by the heavy sack. Bounce a bit in your knees at each step. Don't correct the children when they don't walk in the musical rhythm! Through frequent repetition the older children will get the rhythm into their legs.

8   Stop and patiently wait until all have stopped. Then set down the imaginary sack with a movement to the right with "aah."

9   Make a megaphone with your hands a little in front of your mouth and call the name: "Nicholaus." Take plenty of time; the call is not bound by the rhythm of the song.

80

10 Please also come to
                    our house
11 With your great, big sack!
12 And unpack! –
                    And unpack!

10 As in 2.

11 As in 3.

12 With both hands,
    reach deep into the
    imaginary sack and take
    something out.

Part II: Hand Gesture Games, Songs and Movement Games for Winter

Snowflakes So White

CD track 30

PRELUDE

with Choroi Kinderharp or Choroi glockenspiel

SOFT AND FLOATING   *MELODY: WILMA ELLERSIEK*

It is very suitable to welcome the first snow with the song: *Snowflakes So White.* Perhaps when children and care giver have quietly observed the falling snow, the adult will play on the kinderharp to accompany the falling snow with the prelude of this song. Then the harp may be layed aside and all may sing the song: *Snowflakes So White,* with hand gestures, if possible. For the ending, the adult again can let the harp sound with the music of the postlude.

If it snowed at night for the fist time and the children are full of joy about it, again this happy event can be celebrated with this song. Through the hand gestures the children experience the lightness of an individual snow flake and how easily it can be swayed by any light air currant.

Note:

Instead of the Choroi kinderharp one can play the cantele or a soprano leier. Since both of these instruments are built with a resonance body, the strings should be plucked especially gently. This will protect the sensitive constitution of the very young child up to the seventh year.

If the glockenspiel is used it is best to cover the hammers with a felt cap. This will produce a mild sound, pleasant to the very young child.

84

Snowflakes So White

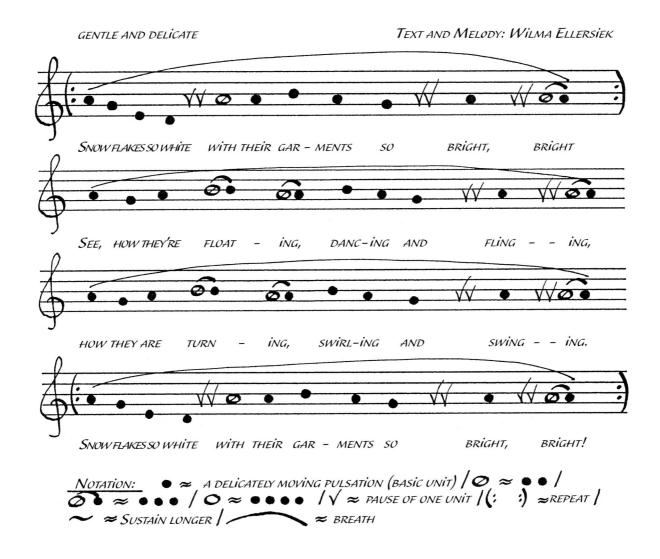

GENTLE AND DELICATE   *TEXT AND MELODY: WILMA ELLERSIEK*

Snow flakes so white with their gar - ments so bright, bright

See, how they're float - ing, danc-ing and fling - - ing,

how they are turn - ing, swirl-ing and swing - - ing.

Snow flakes so white with their gar - ments so bright, bright!

NOTATION: ● ≈ A DELICATELY MOVING PULSATION (BASIC UNIT) / ⊘ ≈ ● ● /
⊘● ≈ ● ● ● / ○ ≈ ● ● ● ● / √ ≈ PAUSE OF ONE UNIT / (: :) ≈ REPEAT /
~ ≈ SUSTAIN LONGER / ⌣ ≈ BREATH

TEXT:

1   Snowflakes so white

HAND GESTURES:

1   Lift your hands, fingers relaxed, above your head before starting to sing. Then, as you sing, move your hands, fingers moving airily, slowly and lightly down. The flakes fall down to about chest height.

85

2 with their garments so
out
bright, bright,
in   *out*
bright, bright.
in   *out*

3 Snowflakes so white with
their garments so bright.

4 See how they're
in
floating, floating,

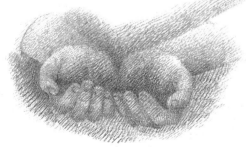

5 dancing and
flinging, flinging,

6 How they are
turning, turning,

2 Both hands, palms down, form little parachutes at chest height. In this "parachute position," both hands rhythmically turn in and out from the wrist. Your hands remain in place at constant height.

3 Repeat 1 and 2.

4 At "see how they," turn both your hands in parachute position inward, one more time; then, at "floating," let the parachutes float up and down, very airily and lightly.

5 Your hands are again at chest height. At the word "dancing," all your fingers wiggle. At "flinging," your hands again assume the parachute position, but with palms up. With a downward swing, move your hands toward each other at "fling," and apart at "ing."

6 Turn "parachute hands," palms down, and make a horizontal circle at chest height for each "turning."

7 swirling and swinging,
            swinging.

8 Snowflakes so white with
   their garments so bright.

9 *silent movement*

10 Softly they have come
             to us.

11 Softly – softly – softly!

7 Hold your hands with open
   fingers (see illustration);
   then, turn your lower arms
   as fast as possible back and
   forth, with hands twirling.
   For "swinging," make the
   same movements as in 5
   for "flinging."

8 Repeat 1 and 2.

9 Lower your hands with
   moving fingers lightly and
   slowly, without singing.
   When your hands have
   arrived on your thighs, the
   table or the floor, the
   movement dies down and
   you look and listen after it.

10 Now start singing
    "Softly they have come
    to us." Your hands
    remain quietly in your lap.
    After the song, move your
    hands slowly and silently
    to your ears.

11 At the first "softly," your
    hands touch your ears and
    you listen. Hold your head
    still during this part; only
    at the last "softly," nod
    very slightly.

Postlude

with Choroi Kinderharp or Choroi glockenspiel

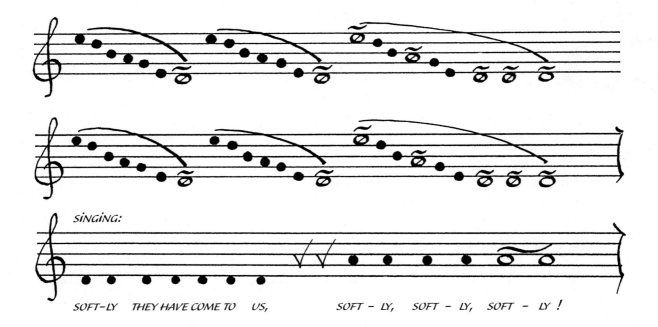

SINGING:

SOFT-LY THEY HAVE COME TO US,   SOFT – LY,   SOFT – LY,   SOFT – LY !

It Snows

It snows – it snows – it snows!
It snows – it snows – it snows!

Far and wide – far and wide –
Wherever I look – snowfields white –
White snow!

Hay-oh! – Hay-oh! – Hay-oh! –
Hay-oh! – Hay-oh! – Hay-oh! –

TEXT:

1   It snows – it snows –
             it snows!
    It snows – it snows –
             it snows!

2   Far and wide –
             far and wide –

HAND GESTURES:

1   Start with your hands slightly above your head, lowering them straight down, parallel to each other, with airily moving fingers and thumbs, until your fingertips touch your thighs. The speed of your movements should be even and the "ow" in "snows" slow, almost singing. For the second line, repeat the same movement, starting again above your head.

2   With the same airy finger gesture, move your parallel hands in a light arc up - first to the left, then to the right. Give yourself time. Again, stretch the vowels in "far," and "wide," almost singing.

3   Wherever I look – snow –
                fields white –

3   At "wherever I look,"
move your hands with the
same finger movements
up and to the sides in
opposite directions, and at
"snowfields white,"
together again, tracing the
same path. Speak the vow-
els slowly.

4   White snow!

4   Now move your parallel
hands up, and at "white,"
let it snow straight down
to your thighs or to the
floor, as in 1. Let the "ow"
in snow sound until your
fingertips have completely
descended. The whole
sequence from 1 to 4
must be experienced as a
breathing action. The
silent direction changes
are important.

5   Hay-oh! – Hay-oh! –
              Hay-oh! –
  Hay-oh! – Hay-oh! –
              Hay-oh! –

5   Lift your hands high and
turn them rhythmically
in and out.

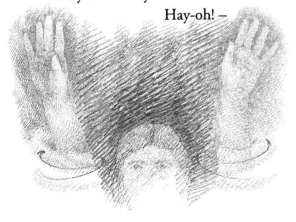

Softly Tippytoe
CD track 31

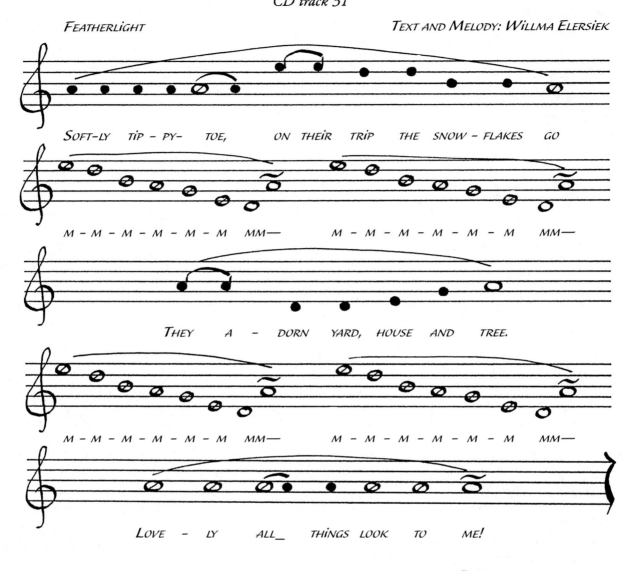

FEATHERLIGHT   TEXT AND MELODY: WILLMA ELERSIEK

Soft-ly tip-py-toe, on their trip the snow-flakes go

M-M-M-M-M-M MM— M-M-M-M-M-M MM—

They a-dorn yard, house and tree.

M-M-M-M-M-M MM— M-M-M-M-M-M MM—

Love-ly all_ things look to me!

NOTATION: ● ≈ ONE PULSATION IN A MIDDLE TEMPO (BASIC UNIT) | ♩♫ ≈ ● FOR ONE PULSE
TWO SHORT LIGHT TONES | ⌀ ≈ ●● | ⌀̑ ≈ ●●● | ○ ≈ ●●●● | ∼ ≈
SUSTAIN LONGER

TEXT:

1 Softly tippytoe,

HAND GESTURES:

1 Lift both hands to the height of your head along the width of your shoulders, your hands loosely open, and your palms turned toward the children. Look up into the "clouds" and very gently

This song is very suitable for greeting the first snow. It also gives a fitting mood for several other winter games from this book and from *GIVING LOVE – BRINGING JOY.* Some examples are: *How the Snowflakes Adorn the Earth, The Snow-Hayoh, Building a*

2 On their trip the snowflakes go.

3 M-m-m-m-m-m-mm-
M-m-m-m-m-m-mm.

4 They adorn yard,

5 House

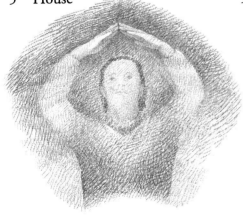

6 and tree.

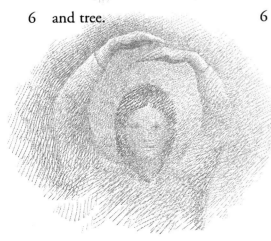

---

tap into the air – first with your left hand at "softly," then with your right hand at "toe."

2 Lift your hands a little higher. Lower your hands with wiggling fingers in a light and airy movement as the "snow."

3 Repeat the movements as in 2 twice more.

4 At "yard," point to the ground with both hands.

5 Form a roof above your head with your arms and hands, your stretched fingers touching each other.

6 At "tree," form a circle with your arms around your head.

Snowman, On the Skating Lake, Glitz – Glitz and Thaws Away, Dreaming of Snowing – of Snow.

GLOCKENSPIEL OR CHOROI BRASS SOUND-TUBES:

Use sound plates or sound-tubes tuned to the fifth interval with central tone A. Cover the head of the striker with felt so that the sound is muted for the children's fine hearing.

In the music, all tones to be struck are marked with "*x.*"

If you are well-versed in the use of the glockenspiel or sound-tubes you may attempt to also include some of the gestures as described. At any rate, sing along. For the end, strike the A once more, move the striker in a large arc, slowly back, and lay it down noiselessly.

7 M-m-m-m-m-m-mm-
M-m-m-m-m-m-mm.

8 Lovely all things look
to me.

A Softly tippytoe,

B On their trip the
snowflakes go.

C

D They adorn yard,
house and tree.

7 Movements as in 2.

8 Move your hands forward
in an arc and then stretch
out at the sides showing
how beautiful the snow-
covered world is.

A. Strike the cymbals lightly
at "softly." At "tippy,"
swing the sounding cym-
bals out, and at "toe,"
swing them back to their
previous position.

B. Repeat the swings out and
in without striking the
cymbals again.

C. After the word "go," strike
the cymbals again. The left
cymbal tips against the right
cymbal from underneath, as
in the illustration. Then
describe an upward arc with
the cymbals returning down
along the outside. Do not
hum the melody during
this movement so that one
can listen to the cymbal
sound. Repeat stroke and
movement together with
the melody.

D. Now sing again. After the
cymbals have arrived from
the upward arc down to
waist height on either side,
tip the cymbals gently
from above at the word
"yard." Tip the cymbals
again at shoulder height

USE OF FINGER CYMBALS:

Hold the finger cymbals at
about chest height.

The song can also be accompanied by finger cymbals of
silver-bronze, using the directions above. Silver finger cymbals can be obtained where
Orff instruments are sold.

with the word "house,"
then raise them to the
height of your head at
"tree," tipping into the air.

E.   As in C.

E

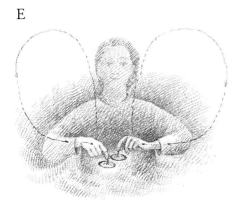

F   Lovely all things look

        to me.

F.   Sing again. At "lovely,"
strike the cymbals again
gently, from top down.
Then move your cymbals
in a large arc forward, and
around horizontally, until
they are together again; let
the sound die out. Repeat
the stroke and movement
once more without singing.

How the Snowflakes Adorn the Earth

SNOWFLAKES CAME FLYING FROM HEAVENLY HEIGHT.
THEY HAVE CLAD THE EARTH IN WHITE.

THE FENCE RECEIVED CAPS, THE ROOF A HAT.
LITTLE CAPS, LARGE HAT.

SNOWFLAKES CAME FLYING FROM HEAVENLY HEIGHT.
THEY HAVE CLAD THE EARTH IN WHITE.

THE GREAT, BIG BARREL WAS GIVEN A COLLAR,
A ROUND, SOFT COLLAR.

SNOWFLAKES CAME FLYING FROM HEAVENLY HEIGHT.
THEY HAVE CLAD THE EARTH IN WHITE.

TREES WERE SNOWED IN FROM TOP TO TOES,
THEY WERE GIVEN THEIR WINTER CLOTHES.

SNOWFLAKES CAME FLYING FROM HEAVENLY HEIGHT.
THEY HAVE CLAD THE EARTH IN WHITE.

THEY COVERED THE MEADOW WARM AND DEEP,
IT WAS GIVEN A BLANKET FOR WINTER SLEEP.

SNOWFLAKES CAME FLYING FROM HEAVENLY HEIGHT.
THEY HAVE CLAD THE EARTH IN WHITE.

TEXT:	HAND GESTURES:
1 Snowflakes came flying from heavenly height.	1 Move your arms and hands above your head. Your hands are open, with relaxed fingers and palms forward, toward the children. To show the gesture of snowing, slowly lower your hands, and move your fingers lightly and airily as snowflakes. Speak at a tempo in which your fingertips touch your

thighs or the floor at the word "height." The speech melody accompanies the movements from top to bottom.

2 They have clad the earth

2 With your hands forward, indicate the ground at the word "earth," as if delicately touching something.

3 in white.

3 Carefully turn your hands, palms upward. With a gentle nod of your head, slowly spread your arms and hands until they are completely open. Speak slowly, with full admiration in your voice for this event of nature. Do all the movements slowly and delicately.

4 The fence received caps,

4 Join your hands at your fingertips and wrists. At the word "cap," both hands meet at chest height, surrounding a hollow place.

5 the roof a hat.

5 At the word "hat," the fingertips of both your hands meet above your head, forming a roof.

6   Little caps, large hat.

7   Snowflakes came flying
      from heavenly height.
   They have clad the earth
          in white.

8   The great, big barrel

6   Repeat movements for the words cap and hat.

7   Repeat hand gestures as in 1, 2 and 3.

8   Form a large, horizontal circle in front of your body with your arms and hands, as if holding a big ball.

9   **was given a collar,**

9   Fold your hands behind your head at the nape of your neck.

10 A round, soft collar.

10 Continue with the gesture of 9, but now comfortably snuggle into the imaginary collar while swinging slightly with your upper body.

11 Snowflakes came flying
       from heavenly height.
    They have clad the earth
           in white.

12 Trees were snowed in from
           top to toes,

11 Repeat hand gestures as in 1, 2 and 3.

12 At the word "trees," stretch your arms and hands upwards, your fingers splayed, as "tree limbs." Your palms face your body. Then start snowing with light, airy finger movements, touching yourself lightly, starting at your head, then at your ears, shoulders, chest and belly.

13 They were given their
winter clothes.

14 Snowflakes came flying
from heavenly height.
They have clad the earth
in white.

15 They covered the meadow
warm and deep,

16 It was given a blanket for
winter sleep.

17 Snowflakes came flying
from heavenly height.
They have clad the earth
in white.

13 Once you have arrived at
your knees with your
snowing movement, stretch
out your arms, and at the
word "winter," turn to the
left, then to the right.

14 Repeat hand gestures as in
1, 2 and 3.

15 Lower your hands down to
your thighs (or the
ground.) Hold your hands
next to each other, palms
down. At "warm," stroke
to the left with both
hands, and at "deep,"
stroke in the opposite
direction as if to smooth a
blanket.

16 Cross your arms before
your chest and comfort-
ably move to and fro in
this position.

17 Repeat hand gestures as in
1, 2 and 3.

The Snow-Hayoh!

CD track 32

HAPPY AND FULL OF ENERGY
(ALLA BREVE)

TEXT AND MELODY BY WILMA ELLERSIEK

SNOW - SNOW - SNOW! FROM HEA-VEN SNOWS THE SNOW!

THE CHILD-REN NOW HAVE LOTS OF FUN, IT'S SNOW-ING, SNOW-ING ON AND ON.

(: SNOW - SNOW - SNOW!- HAY-OH!- HAY-OH!- HAY-OH!- :)

IN-SIDE THE CHILD-REN WILL NOT STAY, THEY RUN OUT-SIDE IN SNOW TO PLAY.

(: SNOW - SNOW - SNOW!- HAY-OH!- HAY-OH!- HAY-OH!- :)

TO START THEY HAVE A SNOWBALL THROW, MAKE QUICKLY MANY BALLS OF SNOW.

(: PLONG! AND PLUNG! HAY-OH!- HAY-OH!- HAY-OH!- :)

AND THEN THEIR SLEDS THEY ALL GET OUT AND WHIZ DOWN-HILL WITH MANY A SHOUT:

Notation: ⊘ ≈ one quiet pulsation (basic unit) / ●● ≈ ⊘ two notes for one pulsation in a flowing tempo / ⊘● ≈ ●●● / (: :) ≈ repeat / ⌢ ≈ sustain longer

TEXT:	HAND GESTURES:
1 Snow – snow – snow! 	1 Turn your raised hands in and out in a lively way, following the speech rhythm, for one turn per syllable.
2 From heaven snows the snow! 	2 Phase the turning movement into a snowing movement. Move your hands, stretched high above your head, straight downward, with your loose and relaxed fingers wiggling, until your fingertips touch your thighs. You may slow down the singing if necessary, so that the snowing movement does not stop until there is a sufficient layer of "snow" on your thighs.

3 The children now have
     x
             lots of fun,
      x   *x*
It's snowing, snowing on
            and on.
	3 At each "*x*," clap your hands softly and airily. At "it's snowing, snowing," lift your hands up again and repeat the snowing movement as described above.

4 Snow – snow – snow!	4 As in 1.

5 Hay-oh! – Hay-oh! –
  x   *x*
         Hay-oh!
       x
	5 At "x," clap softly and airily again.

6 Snow – snow – snow!
   Hay-oh! – Hay-oh! –
         Hay-oh!
	6 Repeat 4 and 5.

7 Inside the children

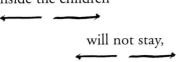

will not stay,

8 they run out in the

. . . .
r / r /

snow to play.

. . .
r / r

9 Snow – snow – snow!
Hay-oh! – Hay-oh! –
Hay-oh!
Snow – snow – snow!
Hay-oh! – Hay-oh! –
Hay-oh!

10 To start, they have a

r   r

snowball throw,

/   /

Make quickly many

r   r

balls of snow.

/   /

11 Plong! And plung!

12 Hay-oh! – Hay-oh! –

x   x

Hay-oh!

x

13 Plong! And plung!
Hay-oh! – Hay-oh! –
Hay-oh!

7 Shake your head in
rhythm – as shown by the
arrows – to and fro as if to
say: "no, no."

8 Taking turns with your
right and left hand "walk"
along your thighs towards
your knees.

9 Repeat 4, 5 and 6.

10 With both hands, make
four snowballs. Press your
hands together twice for
each snowball: for the first
snowball press the snow
twice with your right hand
into your left hand. For the
second snowball press the
snow twice with your left
hand into your right hand.
Repeat this for the third
and fourth snowball. The
hand that presses down on
the other is marked below
the song text.

11 At "plong and plung,"
throw each an imaginary
snowball with your
right hand.

12 At "x," clap softly and airily.

13 Repeat 11 and 12.

14 And then their sleds

        x

      they all get out,

14 Grasp an imaginary rope with both hands to the left behind you. There is a sled tied to the rope. At the word "sled," pull the sled forward with a strong movement.

15 And whiz downhill with

      many a shout.

15 Holding your hands closely together, with palms down and thumbs touching, move them energetically from the upper right to the lower left, down a "steep hill" with the words "whiz" and "many."

16 Ssss – ssss – ssst!

16 Repeat movement as described in 15 for first and third "ssss." For second "ssss," return your hands to their original position.

17 Hay-oh! – Hay-oh! –

   x   *x*

        Hay-oh!

       x

17 Clap at "*x*."

18 Ssss– ssss – ssst!
Hay-oh! – Hay-oh! –

        Hay-oh!

18 Repeat 16 and 17.

19 They build a snowman

     too, you see,

19 Bend forward so that you can touch the floor. First show the lowest, biggest snowball. At "build," press the snow down with both flat hands. At "snowman," show the second snowball, smaller then the lower one. At "too," press down the snow. At "you see," show the snowball for the head and press it down at "a one." The showing of the snowman is a smooth, continuous movement.

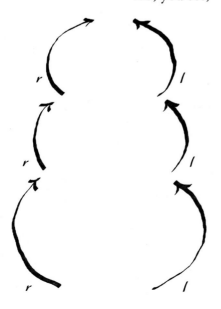

20 One that really laughs
          with me.

20 With a happy, smiling face, form fists at chest height, with pointers sticking straight upward. At "that really," move your pointers to emphasize the text. It's a small, naughty movement. At "laughs with me," open your fists and form a little bowl. Now join your wrists together so that your hands are in opposite positions. Now move your hands closely underneath your chin so that your fingers can enclose your cheeks. Leave a small distance between your hands and your laughing face.

21 Ha! – Ha! – Haah!

21 At "ha! – ha! – haah!" move your "framed" head first to the right, then to the left, then again to the right.

22 Hay-oh! – Hay-oh! –
  x   *x*
             Hay-oh!
          x

22 Clap at "*x*."

23 Ha! – Ha! – Haah!
   Hay-oh! – Hay-oh! –
          Hay-oh!

23 Repeat 21 and 22.

Repeat the beginning of the song with the gestures described in 1-6.

Building a Snowman

Rhythmic-Musical Hand Gesture and Body Movement Game

TODAY WE WANT TO BUILD A SNOWMAN,
YES, A MAN OF SNOW – OF SNOW!

HOOPA* – HOH! HOOPA – HOH!
HOOPA – HOOPA – HOOPA – HOH!

THE SNOW, THE SNOW, WE NEED TO ROLL:
ROLLING – ROLLING – ROLLING – ROLLING,
ROLL A GREAT, BIG, GIANT BALL!
THIS UPON THE GROUND IS STUCK:
HOOPA! – THERE, WE ARE IN LUCK!

ON WE'RE ROLLING – ROLLING – ROLLING:
ROLL A GREAT, BIG, GIANT BALL!
THIS UPON THE TOP IS STUCK:
HOOPA! – THERE, WE ARE IN LUCK!

ON WE'RE ROLLING – ROLLING – ROLLING:
ROLL A – WA-AIT! TOO BIG! INSTEAD,
THIS ONE'S ONLY FOR THE HEAD!
THIS UPON THE TOP IS STUCK:
HOOPA – THERE, WE ARE IN LUCK!

BOB – BOB – BOB – BOB,
PATTING SO THE SNOW GETS HARD,
BOB – BOB – BOB – BOB,
AND NO KNOCK BREAKS IT APART!
BOB – BOB – BOB AND BOB,
BOB – BOB – BOB!

NOW THE SNOWMAN GETS A HAT!
TWO EYES, A LONG NOSE,
AND A MOUTH WE MAKE. YOU SEE –
OUR SNOWMAN LAUGHS WITH ME!

BIG, BIG BUTTONS ON HIS BELLY.
HE PUTS HIS FIST AGAINST HIS SIDE.
THERE! OUR SNOWMAN STANDS ARIGHT!
THEN AT LAST HE GETS A BROOM.
HE IS FINISHED! HOOPA – HOH!
FINISHED IS THE MAN OF SNOW.
HOOPA – HOH! HOOPA – HOH!
HOOPA – HOOPA – HOOPA - HOH!

TEXT:

1   Today we want to build
              a snowman,
    Yes, a man of snow –
              of snow!

2   Hoopa – hoh! Hoopa –

              hoh!

3   Hoopa – hoopa –
        x   x
              hoopa – hoh!
                 x   x

4   The snow, the snow, we
              need to roll:

5   Rolling – rolling – rolling
                    – rolling,

HAND GESTURES:

1   Turn and call joyfully to
    the children.

2   Hold your hands above
    your head and turn them
    in and out in the rhythm
    of the speech.

3   Lightly clap your hands
    in the given rhythm,
    making a small arc
    upwards after each clap,
    then return them to the
    original position.

4   At the word "snow," point
    to the ground with both
    hands. Then return your
    hands in front of you and
    show your fists at "roll."

5   Roll your fists around each
    other in front of your
    body, the right fist forward
    and turning around the

*Pronunciation: The "oo"
vowal in "hooppa" is pro-
nounced short as in "book."

MOVEMENT GAME

This game can also be fun to
play as a movement game.
Stand in the room with the
children loosely grouped
around you. From 1 to 4, all
the gestures are done as
described. At 5, move slowly
forward, bent over, to roll the
snowballs. Also, the circles your
arms describe here get bigger
and bigger.

At 6, pat the floor with the
palms of your hands. Then
carry the snowball to this place
and set it down with "hoopa."
It is important to remember
where the first snowball was set
down so that you are sure to

107

Roll a great, big, giant ball!

O O O O O O

6   This upon the ground
                is stuck:

7   *Silent movement —*
             Hoopa!

8   There, we are in luck!

9   On we're rolling – rolling –
               rolling:
  Roll a great, big, giant ball!
  This upon the top is stuck:
  Hoopa!
  There, we are in luck!

10 On we're rolling – rolling –
              rolling:
  Roll a – wa-ait! –

11 Too big! Instead,

12 This one's only for
           the head!

13 This upon the top is stuck:

---

left fist, toward the children. With each turn, the circles expand. At the end, the left fist turns once more around the right fist, without words. As the circles become larger the speech becomes slower.

6 At "ground," point downward with the fingers of both hands. At "stuck," make an accented movement downward, palms down, with both hands.

7 Grab the heavy, imaginary ball with both arms, pick it up, and at "hoopa," set it down.

8 Rub your hands in satisfaction and nod your head at "luck."

9 Gestures as described in 4 to 8, only the position of the second ball is indicated at a higher place.

10 Beginning gestures are as in 4. At "wa-ait," lift your hands, palms forward and fingers pointing up, toward the children. Hold this gesture a while, then call "wa-ait."

11 Move your hands to and fro several times in a negating gesture.

12 Show an imaginary ball with your hands, at about head height, nodding once at "head."

13 Point at the imaginary snowman with your finger-

---

put the other snowballs on top. The patting can be done on the imaginary snowman or on your own body. In either case, follow the sequences as described in 15. After that, all movements are done on your own body while standing still.

108

14 *Silent movement* —
Hoopa!
There, we are in luck!
15 B<u>o</u>b – b<u>o</u>b – b<u>o</u>b – b<u>o</u>b,
P<u>a</u>tting <u>s</u>o the sn<u>ow</u>
                        gets h<u>a</u>rd,
B<u>o</u>b – b<u>o</u>b – b<u>o</u>b – b<u>o</u>b,
<u>A</u>nd no kn<u>o</u>ck breaks
                        <u>it</u> ap<u>a</u>rt!
B<u>o</u>b – b<u>o</u>b – b<u>o</u>b and b<u>o</u>b,
B<u>o</u>b – b<u>o</u>b – b<u>o</u>b!

tips, this time at about head height, and don't accentuate the downward movement at "stuck" as much as the time before.

14 As in 7 and 8, only at a higher position. Carry the small ball with your hands.

15 Now, pat the snow hard with flat hands at the rhythm indicated by the underlined syllables. At your head, pat more slowly and lightly in the indicated sequence; begin in the front, then behind, then temples and cheeks. Then, pat down your body in a livelier way. At the height of your collarbone, pat in the middle, then the outside. Follow this gestural pattern, patting in the middle and then the outside, at the height of your breastbone, chest, stomach, upper belly and lower belly. At the end, pat again, moving upwards. At your lower belly and upper belly, pat in the middle and then the outside. At your stomach, breast and breastbone, pat only in the middle and at a slower speed. It is important that you demonstrate the sequence exactly, down and up again, patting in the middle and on the outside. The children will imitate as they can. Don't correct them.

16 Now the snowman gets

        a hat!

16 Lift both hands up. By "a," the fingertips of your pointer, middle and ring fingers touch. At "hat," move your hands downward and set the hat on your head. Speak slowly and show the hat for a while.

17 Two eyes,

17 Put your fists with the middle section of your fingers on your eyes.

18 a long nose,

18 Hold your fists, one in front of the other, in front of your nose.

19 And a m<u>ou</u>th we m<u>a</u>ke.

        You s<u>ee</u> -

19 With the thumbs and pointers of both your hands, hold small, imaginary pebbles. Your other fingers are rolled in. From the middle of your lips to the outer corners of your mouth, set in the little "pebbles" in the indicated speech rhythm. Touch your own mouth only very lightly, so that the children can understand what you say.

20 Our snowman laughs

        with me!

20 At "our," stick your pointers out from your fists, holding your hands so closely together that they almost touch. At the word "snowman," turn your fists so that your pointers touch each other at the middle of your lips. Now, draw the arc of the laughing lips even beyond the corners of your mouth as you say "laughs," and laugh at the children.

21 Big, big buttons on
    his belly.

22 He puts his fist against
    his side.

23 There! Our snowman
    stands aright!

24 Then at last he gets
    a broom.
    He is finished!
    Hoopa – hoh!
    Finished is the man
    of snow.

25 Hoopa – hoh!
    o   o
    Hoopa – hoh!
    o   o

26 Hoopa – hoopa –
    x   x
    hoopa - hoh!
    x   x

21 In the given speech rhythm,
   put your fists, with the
   middle fingers against your
   chest, in a line downward
   to show the "buttons."

22 Place your fists against
   your sides.

23 Make yourself wide,
   and laugh.

24 Hold your right arm high
   above your head, your fingers spread as the
   "broom." In this position
   call joyfully to the children: "He is finished!"

25 Hold your hands up and
   loosely turn them from
   your wrists.

26 Clap as in 3. After the
   last clap, make a larger
   arc upward as your
   final gesture.

Oh, David's Star

CD track 33

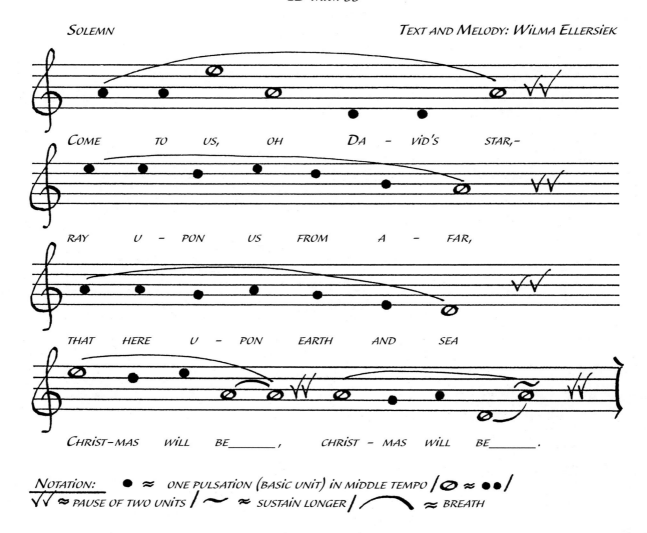

SOLEMN

TEXT AND MELODY: WILMA ELLERSIEK

COME TO US, OH DA - VID'S STAR,-

RAY U - PON US FROM A - FAR,

THAT HERE U - PON EARTH AND SEA

CHRIST-MAS WILL BE____, CHRIST - MAS WILL BE____.

NOTATION: ● ≈ ONE PULSATION (BASIC UNIT) IN MIDDLE TEMPO / ⊘ ≈ ●● /
∨∨ ≈ PAUSE OF TWO UNITS / ～ ≈ SUSTAIN LONGER / ⌒ ≈ BREATH

TEXT:

1 Come to us,
      oh, David's star,

HAND GESTURES:

1 Hold your hands in front of your head, with fingers spread, one behind the other, and palms forward. Slide the spread fingers of your left hand into the gaps between the fingers of your right hand, both thumbs sticking out at the sides. Move the star gesture straight up.

2 Ray upon us from afar.

2 Tilt the star slightly forward, moving it down to about neck height.

3 That here upon
      earth and sea,

3 Dissolve the star gesture. Moving your hands downward in an arc, point to the earth.

4 Christmas will be!

4 Lift your hands and lower arms, palms outward, next to your head. They are the wings of the angel who brings the glad tidings. At "will be," the wings make a small movement forward and back, a light wing stroke.

5 Christmas will be!

5 Lower your hands and arms toward the front, palms down, in a gesture of blessing. At the last syllable, lift your hands again lightly; see the upper hand position in the picture. Hold this gesture for a while.

Christmas Call

CD track 34

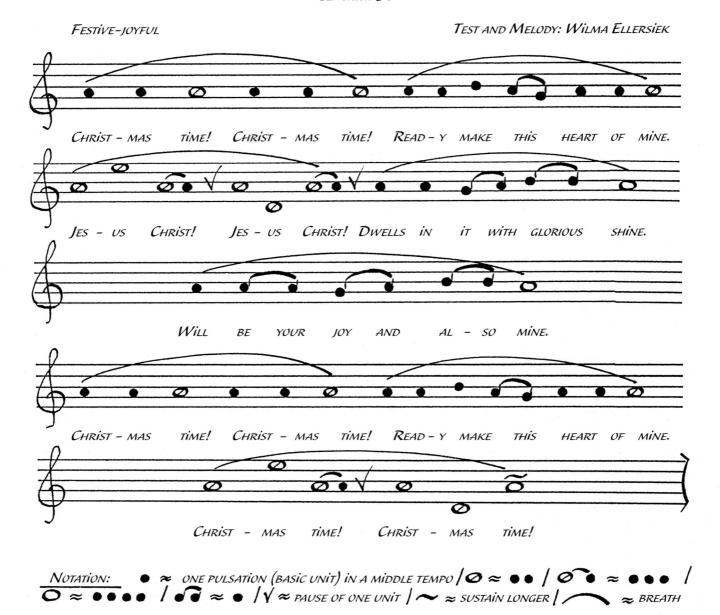

Festive-joyful

Test and Melody: Wilma Ellersiek

Christ - mas time! Christ - mas time! Read - y make this heart of mine.

Jes - us Christ! Jes - us Christ! Dwells in it with glorious shine.

Will be your joy and al - so mine.

Christ - mas time! Christ - mas time! Read - y make this heart of mine.

Christ - mas time! Christ - mas time!

Notation: ● ≈ ONE PULSATION (BASIC UNIT) IN A MIDDLE TEMPO | ∅ ≈ ●● | ∅͡● ≈ ●●● | ∅ ≈ ●●●● | ♪♪ ≈ ● | √ ≈ PAUSE OF ONE UNIT | ～ ≈ SUSTAIN LONGER | ⌣ ≈ BREATH

114

On the Skating Lake

It froze so hard the whole night long.
It made the ice quite thick and strong
On the skating lake.
Quickly, the children take
Their skates and put them on.

Now they're gliding light and nice,
Light and nice upon the ice,
Fast they move ahead.
Light and nice, light and nice,
Fast they move ahead.
Stop instead.

Turn quickly in a pirouette,
Pirouette – pirouette,
Pirou – pirou – pirouette.
Whoosh! – They sit upon their tush!
That does not hurt.

The children all stand up again.
Glide again now, light and nice,
Light and nice upon the ice,
Fast they move ahead.
Light and nice, light and nice,
Fast they move ahead.
Stop instead!

Enough for today.
Change their shoes; the skating's done.
Quickly, quickly home they run.
Quickly, quickly home they run.

TEXT:	HAND GESTURES:
1 It froze so hard the whole night long.	1 By looking at you, one can see that you are freezing and that it is cold. Rub your hands to warm them; at "it froze," rub the top of your left hand with your right hand several times, and at "whole night long," rub your right hand with your left hand.
2 It made the ice quite thick and strong	2 To find out if the ice is really frozen solid, press down on your thighs with both hands, flat and together. First press on your upper thighs, then in the middle, and finally, close to your knees at the words "ice," "thick" and "strong."
3 On the skating lake.	3 Place your hands, palms down and close together, in front of you just above your thighs. Now, move your hands apart and toward your sides to indicate a lake lying in front of you. Then bring them together again, meeting directly in front of your body above your thighs.
4 Quickly, the children take	4 Hold your right hand just above your thighs, hand and fingers stretched and fingertips pointing toward the children. The rim of your pinky faces downward. With your left hand, enclose your pinky, and at "children take," rub along from your pinky tip to your wrist.

5   Their skates and put
    them on.

6   Now they're gliding light
    r   *l*   *r*
                     and nice,
                              l
    Light and nice upon
    r   *l*   *r*
                         the ice,
                                 l
    Fast they move ahead.
    r   *l*   *r*   *l*
    Light and nice, light
    r   *l*   *r*
                         and nice,
                                  l
    Fast they move ahead.
    r   *l*   *r*   *l*

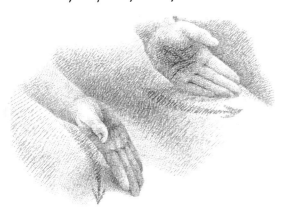

7   Stop instead.

5   The same gesture as
    in 4, but your hands
    are exchanged.

6   Your vertically held hands
    are now the "skates,"
    sliding rhythmically on the
    pinkies. They turn right
    and left across your thighs,
    the "ice." Both speech and
    movement accelerate.

7   At "stop," move both
    hands parallel, slanting
    forward to the left and
    coming to a stand by
    making a sudden turn to
    the right.

8 Turn quickly in

a pirouette,

Pirouette – pirouette,

Pirou – pirou – pirouette.

8 Leave your left hand at your side; it does not participate in the pirouette. Lift your right upper arm so that your right hand, fingertips down, hangs freely above your right thigh. Now your right hand circles rhythmically, starting slowly and gaining speed. In preparation for the next movement, lift your hand to head height after the last pirouette and make a fist.

9 Whoosh! – They sit upon their tush!

9 Now drop the right fist, with an accent on "whoosh," down on your right thigh (rolled-in fingers touch your thigh.) Leave your fist lying on your thigh, while nodding at the word "sit." Nod again at "tush," pressing your fist again on your thigh.

10 That does not hurt.

10 Shake your head "no."

11 The children all stand up again.

11 Use your left hand again as you bring both hands into skating position on your thighs.

12 Glide again now, light and nice,
Light and nice upon the ice,
Fast they move ahead.
Light and nice, light and nice,
Fast they move ahead.

12 Exactly as in 6.

13 Stop instead!

13 As in 7.

14 Enough for today.

14 Nod your head at "today."

15 Change their shoes; the skating's done.

15 As in 4, but in reverse direction. With your left hand, slide along the pinky

16 Quickly, quickly home

$\dot{-}$ $\dot{-}$ $\dot{-}$ $\dot{-}$ $\dot{-}$
r   /   r   /   r

            they run.

                $\dot{-}$
                /

Quickly, quickly home

$\dot{-}$ $\dot{-}$ $\dot{-}$ $\dot{-}$ $\dot{-}$
r   /   r   /   r

            they run.

                $\dot{-}$
                /

from the wrist to the tip, and then do the same with your other hand.

16 With flat hands, "walk" in turn on your thighs. Start close to your body and walk to your knees. Speech and movement accelerate.

What Do Animals Do in Snow

Polar Bear
Rhythmic-Musical Body Gesture Game

THE POLAR BEAR, WHAT DOES HE THERE?
GRUM – GRUM – GRUM – GRUM,
THROUGH THE SNOW HE LUMBERS ON,
GRUM –GRUM – GRUM – GRUM.

COMES BITTER COLD, HE STARTS TO DIG
A DEEP PIT INTO THE SNOW:
DIG – DIG – DIG – DIG –
AND SITS DOWN IN THE HOLE,
COVERED WITH SNOW FROM HEAD TO SOLE.

BUT THE HOLE IS STILL OPEN WIDE.
GRUMBLES THE POLAR BEAR: GRUM – GRUM –
GRUM – GRUM. WIND, COME ON,
AND BLOW – BLOW THE HOLE SHUT TIGHT.

PHHH! – PHHH! – COMES A WIND-BLAST.
PHHH! – PHHH! – BLOWS DOWN FAST.
PHHH! – PUTT! – BLOWS ALL SHUT.

THE POLAR BEAR SITS WARM AND SOFT,
ONLY HIS NOSE STICKS OUT ALOFT.
GRUM – GRUM. THANK YOU, DEAR WIND.
GRUM – GRUM – GRUM.

TEXT:

1   The polar bear, what does
    he there?

MOVEMENTS:

1   This is a large motor
    game. Stand in the room,
    with the children around
    you in a loose group.
    Stand with your legs
    apart and your hands
    lifted to chest height as
    "paws." Pose the question
    to the children, slightly

The two additional games
under the heading: *What Do
Animals Do in Snow, Little
Mice in the Snow* and *Birdie
in the Snow* can be played
together with the Polar Bear
game. In all three games we
have a combination of hand
gestures, body gestures and
movements.

120

lowering your head at "what," then lift it again at "he." Speak slowly, with a dark voice, but not pressed down.

2 Grum – grum –
       /   r
            grum – grum,
              /   r

2 Remain standing in the same posture, but now switch your body weight to the left, the right, again the left, and once more to the right. Accompany these movements with "grum – grum," in a dark voice.

3 Through the snow he
       /   r
            lumbers on,
                /   r
   Grum – grum –
       /   r
            grum – grum,
              /   r

3 Now start clumsily moving forward. Lift your legs a little higher than necessary, as the "snow" is deep.

4 Comes bitter cold,

4 The "polar bear" stops, pulling his paws tighter against his chest.
   He is cold.

5 he starts to <u>dig</u>
   a <u>deep</u> <u>pit</u> into the <u>snow</u>:

5 The polar bear bends down and with both hands digs a hole into the snow. Start each movement a little deeper than the previous one: first start at thigh level, then knee, calf and ankle. Each movement should coincide with one of the underlined words.

6 Dig – dig – dig – dig –
      r   /   r   /

6 The polar bear stands with legs apart and digs in turn with his right and left "front paws." Push the snow toward yourself between your knees and

your ankles or between your legs. As you dig, bend your upper body deeper.

7   *silent movement*

7   The polar bear stands up, paws against chest, looks at his "hole" and nods his head.

8   And sits down in the hole,

8   The polar bear slowly drops down on his four legs. At "sits," he turns around, and at "down," he sits on the floor inside his hole.

9   Covered with snow from head to sole.

9   Wrap front paws around back paws (knees pulled up). The polar bear sits this way for a while and snuggles down.

10 But the hole is still **open** wide.

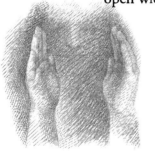

10 At the words "but the hole" the polar bear lifts his head looking slowly up and down. Then he shows the open hole with his front paws shaking his head "no!"

11 Grumbles the polar bear: grum – grum – Grum – grum. Wind, come on,

11 The polar bear returns his paws to his chest and grunts, swinging his upper body lightly to left and right. At "wind," he waves the wind to himself with his front paws.

12 And blow – blow
        r   */*
        the hole shut tight.

12 At "blow – blow," fetch the wind once with the right and then left paw. At "hole," show the hole

13 Phhh! – Phhh! –
      r   /

      Comes a wind-blast.
       r *and*   /

Phhh! – Phhh! –
    r   /

      Blows down fast.
      r   *and*   /

14 Phhh! –
   r and /

   pu-u-u-utt!

15 Blows all shut.

16 The polar bear sits warm
               and soft,

17 Only his nose sticks
               out aloft.

once more with both paws, and at "tight," close paws together.

13 At "Phhh! – Phhh!" again fetch the wind from left and right, and at "comes a wind blast," and "blows down fast," fetch the wind with both paws together.

14 At "phhh," fetch the wind with both paws for the last time. Before the "putt," open wide once more, speak the "pu-u-u-utt" with an extended vowel sound, continue the fetching gesture until your arms are crossed at your chest. Make the movement slowly and with purpose.

15 Continue the movement by lifting your elbows, your hands slipping down your upper arm to your elbow joint. Hold your arms high enough so that your nose can rest on them and you can just see across.

16 Continue gesture 15.

17 Dissolve the gesture and form a nose with both

hands around your own nose. Don't make it too tight; you need to be able to easily breathe and speak.

18 Grum – grum.
        Thank you, dear wind.
    Grum – grum – grum.

18 Lift "nose" a little while you speak. At "thank you," lower your head slightly, then lift it again while rumbling more slowly and softly. Again, lower your head until your elbows rest on your thighs. Continue sitting for a while in this position.

Little Mice in the Snow
Rhythmic-Musical Movement Game

THE LITTLE MICE, WHAT DO THEY DO?
"FEEEEP! – FEEEEP!"
"FEEEEP! – FEEEEP!"
UNDER THE SNOW: SCRATCHY-SCRAPE, SCRATCHY-SCRAPE,
SCRATCHY-SCRATCHY-SCRATCHY-SCRAPE, THEY BUILD AN ESCAPE!
SCRATCHY-SCRATCHY-SCRATCHY-SCRAPE.

STRAIGHT AHEAD – RIGHT AND LEFT THEY GO,
"FEEEEP! – FEEEEP!"

TRIPPING, TRIPPING TO AND FRO, TO AND FRO.
HUSTLE – HUSTLE! – FLIT AND GO!
"FEEEEP! – FEEEEP!"
DANCING – DANCING TIPPYTOE:
DIDDLEDIDDLEDIDDLEDOE – ROUND THEY GO,
DANCING AND TWIRLING, A MOUSY-TWIRLING,
THEIR TAILS A-CURLING, ALL AROUND –
ALL AROUND.

HI! –
THE MICE ARE SPRINGING, HAY-OH – HAY-OH!
SPRINGING – SPRINGING, HI! – HAY-OH!
"FEEEEP! – FEEEEP!" UNDER THE SNOW.

AND THEN AT NIGHT?
THE LITTLE MICE, THEY SNUGGLE DEEP
INTO THEIR SNOW-HOUSE NEST:
"FEEEEP! – FEEEEP! THANK YOU, DEAR SNOW –
"FEEEEP!"
AND THEN THEY REST – AND FALL ASLEEP.

TEXT:

1 The little mice, what do
they do?

2 "Feeeep! – Feeeep!"
"Feeeep! – Feeeep!"

3 Under the snow:

4 **Scratchy-scrape,**
scratchy-scrape,
Scratchy-scratchy-
scratchy-scrape,
5 they build an escape!

MOVEMENTS:

1 Stand before the children
with slightly bent knees
and your hands against
your chest as "paws."

2 In the "mouse-gesture,"
run to and fro in the
room with small steps in
sudden, quick movements
calling "feeeep – feeeep."
Don't imitate the
naturalistic squeak of a
mouse, but use a long,
high musical tone.

3 Kneel down, holding
your arms over your head
like a "dome."

4 With your fingers,
scratch on the floor.
One may hear your
fingernails scraping.
5 Kneel upright, your
hands as paws, with
slightly curled fingers
against your chest as in 1,

6	Scratchy-scratchy- scratchy-scrape.		looking down on the floor. The floor is so to speak – the workplace of the mice.
7	Straight ahead –	6	Scratch again as in 4.
		7	Set your flat hands, on the edge of your pinkies, on the floor, with your palms facing each other and close to your knees. Then, move your hands forward together across the floor, as far away from your body as possible.
8	right and left they go	8	While holding that gesture, move your hands across the floor.
9	"Feeeep! – Feeeep!"	9	Kneeling upright as in 5, call "feeeep – feeeep" in a light, high voice.
10	*silent*	10	Stand up and assume a mouse gesture, as in 1.
11	Tripping, tripping to and fro, to and fro.	11	Move as in 2, making noticeable shifts in direction. Call out "to" and "fro" long and almost singing.
12	Hustle – hustle! – Flit and go!	12	Now run very quickly, speaking in a clipped and short manner. For "hustle-hustle," move in one direction; for "flit and go," in a different direction.
13	"Feeeep! – Feeeep!"	13	Stop suddenly, calling "feeeep" in a high voice.

14	Dancing – dancing
	       tippy-toe:
	Diddlediddlediddledoe –
	      round they go,
		14	In the mouse gesture, stand on tiptoes and slowly turn around. Move slowly, with very small steps, lifting your feet a little higher than

15 Dancing and twirling,
　　/　　　r
a m<u>ou</u>sy-tw<u>i</u>rling,
　　/　　　r

16 Their tails a-curling,

17 all around – all around.

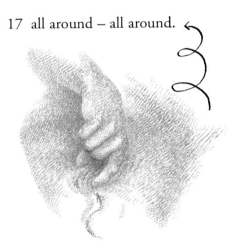

18 Hi! –The mice are
　　springing,

19 hay-oh – hay-oh!
　　Springing – springing, hi!
　　　　　– Hay-oh!

necessary before setting
them down. Arrange the
turning so that there is
only one complete turn
for the text.

15 In the mouse gesture,
starting with the left foot,
delicately lift your feet,
alternating them while
standing. The rhythm of
the movement is
indicated by the
underlined vowels.

16 Move an imaginary tail
from behind you and pull
it to the right, about
waist height.

17 Now form your right
hand into a loose fist
with your pointer sticking
out. Hold your fist so
that your finger points to
the floor. Then, draw two
loops upward with your
finger, next to your body.

18 Again position your
hands as paws, quickly
bending your knees and
preparing to jump. At
"springing," make a big
jump forward into the
room. After the jump,
continue tripping along
in the mouse position.

19 For each word, take a big
jump, taking short steps in
between to slow the
momentum. The rhythm is
free. It is important that
you execute this demanding

	movement without getting short of breath. At the last "hay-oh," take the final jump with both feet. Then, stand still.
20 "Feeeep! – Feeeep!"	20 In the mouse position, call a long "feeeep." After a longer pause, call another "feeeep." Take as much time as you need to catch your breath again. Then, kneel down.
21 under the snow.	21 As in 3.
22 And then at night?	22 Now sit on your heels while lowering your arms and laying them on your thighs.

23 The little mice, they
     snuggle deep
Into their snow-house nest:
"Feeeep! – Feeeep!
    Thank you, dear snow –
Feeeep!"
And then they rest –
     and fall asleep.
	23 There are two possibilities:
	i. Lean a little forward and rest your face – forehead, eyes and cheekbones – in your hands as in a bowl. For breathing and speaking, your nose and mouth must remain free. Speak the "thank you" to the snow in this position. Then, let the two last "feeeeps" peter out.
	ii. Roll slowly to the side and curl up tightly on the floor. Snuggle your head into your bent arms and say the "thank you" in this position.

24 *Sing: "It is Enough!"*	24 Start softly singing the Rest-Fifth Song, and very unobtrusively rise to your knees to sing to the children.

After singing the words of the song, repeat, by humming it. During this humming, rise and stroke the back or side of the "little mouse" lying next to you, continuing on from child to child. If there are more then eight children in the group, it is advisable to stroke two children at the same time so it does not take too long. Repeat the melody as needed. If parents are present, the children can snuggle up to them. Then the parent rocks the child softly during the song and strokes his or her back.

It Is Enough
CD track 35

It is e-nough! It is e-nough!_ ALL THE MICE BOTH

BIG AND SMALL ARE TIRED FROM DAN-CING AND SLEEP ALL.

Observe what the children need. They might still want to lie quietly for a while. If you have the impression that the children would like to repeat the game, rise to your feet, rub your eyes, and sing the "rested now" call.

REST-ED NOW, REST-ED NOW THE LIT-TLE MICE HAVE REST-ED NOW!

Birdie in the Snow
Rhythmic-Musical Movement Game

WHAT DOES THE BIRDIE DO?

THE BIRDIE, TEWIT – TEWIT – CHEEP – CHEEP!

TEWIT – TEWIT – CHEEP – CHEEP!

LOOKS FOR A FEEDER TRAY.

IT WINGS – WINGS – WINGS AWAY.

WINGS – WINGS – WINGS,

WINGS – WINGS – WINGS,

LOOKS FOR A FEEDER TRAY.

THE BIRDIE WINGS – WINGS – WINGS,

SEES THE FEEDER TRAY,

FLIES THERE TO FEED,

FINDS MANY A GOOD SEED.

PECK – PECK – PECK – PECK – PECK – PECK – PAY,

IT PECKS ALL THE SEEDS AWAY,

PECK – PECK – PAY,

ALL AWAY!

THE BIRDIE, TEWIT – TEWIT – CHEEP – CHEEP!

TEWIT – TEWIT – CHEEP – CHEEP!

HAS ENOUGH!

WINGS – WINGS – WINGS THROUGH THE AIR,

WINGS – WINGS TO HIS DWELLING NEAR,

WINGS – WINGS BACK TO HIS NEST.

SNUGGLES INTO ITS WARM NEST: "CHEEP – CHEEP!

THANK YOU FOR THE GOOD SEEDS! CHEEP!"

AND FROM ITS PECKING IT MUST REST, MUST REST

TEXT:	MOVEMENTS:
1 "What does the birdie do?"	1 Turn to the children and ask them this question, perhaps adding: "in the snow."

2   The birdie,

2   With your right hand,
    form a beak with your
    pointer and thumb. Your
    other fingers are loosely
    rolled into a fist.

3   tewit – tewit –
    <<<<   <<<<
                cheep – cheep!
                  <   <
    Tewit – tewit –
    <<<<   <<<<
                cheep – cheep!
                  <   <

3   At "tewit," the little
    beak makes tiny, fast
    movements. At "cheep –
    cheep," open wide and
    close the beak twice.

4   Looks for a feeder tray.

4   Joining your hands with
    your palms up, show a
    "tray" in front of your chest.

5   It wings – wings –

5   Spread your arms wide as
    "wings." The flying
    movement originates at
    your elbows; your loosely
    open hands follow the
    moving impulse
    passively. Feel the air
    drafting past your
    fingertips – then you
    have a lively-looking
    movement. On each of
    the "wings," the wings
    move up and down once.

6   wings away.

6   Rise with a big wing beat.
    Speak the word "wing"
    slowly, almost singing.

7   Wings – wings – wings,
    Wings – wings – wings,
    Looks for a feeder tray.

7   Glide quickly through the
    room as if carried by the
    air, arms up and down for
    each of the "wings."

The birdie wings –
       wings – wings,
Sees the feeder tray,

Direction is "sun-wise;" that is, your right shoulder points to the center of the room. The movement need not be along the circle line. Speak very melodiously, but not all the time. The movement, however, does not stop.

8 Flies there to feed,

8 With a large wing beat, crouch down, moving your arms close to your body. Your left hand lies against your tailbone as the little tail; move your right hand forward and form a little beak at about the height of your knees, as in 2.

9 Finds many a good seed.

9 At "seed," move the little beak down to the floor. If crouching is uncomfortable for you, slowly change to sit on your heels, but leave your left hand in the back as the tail.

10 Peck – peck – peck –
   ·   ·   ·
  peck – peck – peck – pay,
  ·   ·   ·   ·
It pecks all the seeds away.
· · · · ·
Peck – peck – peck –
  ·   ·   ·
  peck – peck – peck – pay,
  ·   ·   ·   ·
It pecks all the seeds away,
· · · · ·
Peck – peck – pay,
  ·   ·   ·

10 Slowly pick up one little seed after the other. The little beak moves exactly in the speech rhythm, at each "·." The tip of the beak touches the floor, and a pause is made each time at the end of the line. At the last line, double the interval between pecks. Don't correct children who cannot peck exactly in the rhythm; it will be established by frequent repetition.

11 All away!

11 Spread your hands, palms up, as if to say: "all gone!"

12 The birdie,
13 tewit – tewit –

<<<<   <<<<

   cheep – cheep!

      <   <

Tewit – tewit –

<<<<   <<<<

   cheep – cheep!

      <   <

12 As in 2.
13 As in 3.

14 Has enough!

14 From your wrist, slowly move the beak up and down as if to say: "I'm full!"

15 Wings – wings –

15 Spread your arms wide again (if you were sitting on your heels, go back into a crouch.) Still crouching, swing your wings lightly up and down.

16 wings through the air,
   Wings – wings –
   to his dwelling near,
   Wings – wings – wings,
   Wings – wings – wings,

16 Arise with a large wing beat and fly away, as in 6 and 7.

17 Back to its nest.

17 With a large wing beat, return to your place (chair, stool) and sit down. Continue repeating the words: "back to its nest," until the last "little bird" has arrived at his or her place.

18 Snuggles into its
              warm nest:

"Cheep – cheep!
      <   <

Thank you for the
      <   <

good seeds! Cheep!"
           <   <

19 And from its pecking it
              must rest – must rest!

20 *See song on page 137.*

18 Form a nest with your left hand and snuggle the right hand with the beak into it. The beak looks out beyond the nest.

While still in the nest, open and close your beak at: "cheep-cheep-thank you," as shown in the left column.

19 Hold the nest with the birdie very quietly and look at it lovingly.

20 While singing, gently rock the nest with the birdie. At "and falls asleep," the little beak disappears into the nest. At the last "and falls asleep," hold both hands still and lay your cheek against the bird in a caress. Hold this gesture for a while.

Wind Rockabye
CD track 36

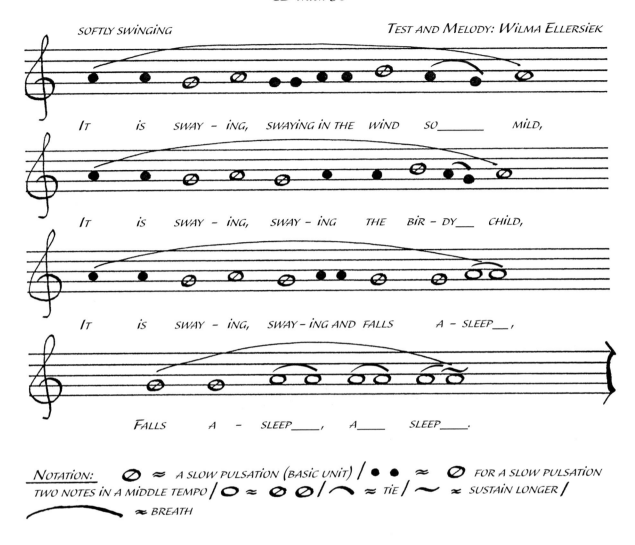

SOFTLY SWINGING

TEST AND MELODY: WILMA ELLERSIEK

It   is   sway - ing,   swaying in the   wind   so_____   mild,

It   is   sway - ing,   sway - ing   the   bir - dy___   child,

It   is   sway - ing,   sway - ing and falls   a - sleep__ ,

FALLS   a   -   sleep____ ,   a____   sleep____ .

NOTATION: ⊘ ≈ A SLOW PULSATION (BASIC UNIT) / ● ● ≈ ⊘ FOR A SLOW PULSATION
TWO NOTES IN A MIDDLE TEMPO / ○ ≈ ⊘ ⊘ / ⌒ ≈ TIE / ～ ≈ SUSTAIN LONGER /
⌣ ≈ BREATH

Snowflake Song

CD track 37

Light but Staid

Text and Melody: Wilma Ellersiek

I'M A LITT - LE SNOW-FLAKE BRIGHT, WEAR AN i - CY GOWN OF WHITE

FLOAT - ING DOWN SO LIGHT AND FREE, SOON UP- ON THE EARTH TO BE.

I'M A WHITE SNOW - FLAKE CHILD, TURN IN THE WIND MILD___,

TURN-ING A - LOFT SO LIGHT_____ AND SOFT_____.

I'M A LITT - LE SNOW-FLAKE BRIGHT, WEAR AN i - CY GOWN OF WHITE

FLOAT - ING DOWN SO LIGHT AND FREE, SOON UP- ON THE EARTH TO BE.

SNOW - ING DOWN FROM HEA - VEN HIGH DOWN, DOWN TO THE EARTH i FLY,

FLOA - TING, FLOA-TING UP AND DOWN, UP AND DOWN, SINK-ING TO THE EARTH, SO BROWN.

138

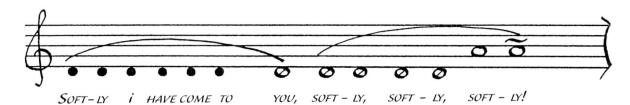

SOFT - LY i HAVE COME TO YOU, SOFT - LY, SOFT - LY, SOFT - LY!

NOTATION: ● ≈ ONE PULSATION (BASIC UNIT) | ♪♩ ≈ ● TWO MOVING NOTES FOR ONE UNIT |

∅ ≈ ● ● | ⊘̃ ● ≈ ● ● ● | ○ ≈ ● ● ● ● | ∼ ≈ SUSTAIN LONGER |

⏜ ≈ BREATH

TEXT:

1 I'm a little snowflake bright,
   Wear an icy gown of white,

   Floating down so light
                        and free,
   Soon upon the earth to be.

2 I'm a white snowflake child,

3 Turn in the wind mild,

   Turning aloft

HAND GESTURES:

1 Your right hand is the snowflake. Hold your hand in front of your chest, palm down, your hand loosely curled like a little parachute. From this position, move the "snowflake" gently and softly up and down according to the melody. Change this up and down movement only at the words "gown of white." Instead, turn your right hand from your wrist to the right and the left. Then follow the melody again; slowly lowering your hand until at the word "earth," you have almost reached your thighs or the floor.

2 Raise your right hand, your snowflake, just above your head at the light vowel "i" in "white," then at "snowflake child," lower it to chest height.

3 The snowflake turns in a horizontal circle once per line as shown.

139

So light and soft.

4   I'm a little snowflake bright,
    Wear an icy gown of white,
    Floating down so light
                    and free,
    Soon upon the earth to be.

5   Snowing from the
                heavens high,
    Down, down to the earth
                        I fly,
    Floating, floating up and
            down, up and down,
    Sinking to the earth,
                    so brown.

6   Softly I have come to you,
    Softly, softly, softly!

4   As in 1.

5   The snowflake still floats
    up and down according
    to the melody. At "so
    brown," it sinks down to
    your thighs or the floor.
    Now turn your hand
    over, palm up, and let it
    rest there.

6   With your left hand
    against your ear listen in
    the direction of the
    resting snowflake. At the
    next three "softlys,"
    slowly dissolve the
    listening gesture, and at
    the end nod lightly with
    your head.

Ribbon Wand

Materials:

Dowel, 1/4" wide, 12" long, per wand
Roll of 4" wide crepe paper
Scotsch tape

All materials for making a ribbon wand are available in craft stores. Dowels are usually available in 4' length, crepe paper streamers in many colors.

Craft Directions:

Cut dowel in the right length, smoothing cut ends with sand paper. Cut four lengths of crepe paper, 13" long. Cut in half lengthwise, so that there are eight 2" wide ribbons.

The ribbons are fastened to the end of the dowel with 3/4" wide clear tape. Cut a 6" piece of, Scotsch tape. Lay dowel on the Scotsch tape 1" from the end at a right angle so that the end of the dowel is equal with the rim of the tape. Now fasten the eight ribbons onto the, Scotsch tape in a row, in opposite direction from the dowel but only to the middle of the tape. Starting with the dowel, roll up dowel and ribbons, pressing the glue end tightly on the dowel.

When the ribbons are attached, cut each in half lengthwise to 1" of tape so that there are sixteen narrow ribbons. Choose lively colors for the ribbons. Store the wands in a long, narrow basket and cover them with a light cloth.

Jingle Stick

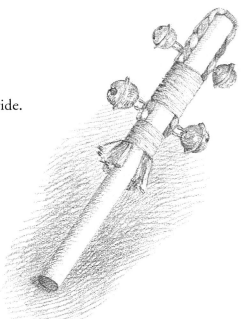

Materials:

Dowel, 5/8" wide, 6"long, per stick.
Raffia or colored braid, 1 1/2" wide or 2 pieces, 3/4" wide.
4 brass jingles, 2 each with Ø 1/2" and Ø 3/4".
Round elastic.

Use jingles with metal balls as the tone producer. Larger jingles should not be used; their sound is too dominating.

Brass jingles with inner balls of metal are available at; Nova Natural Toys and Crafts, see addresses on page148. They may also be for sale at the school store of your local Waldorf school.

Craft Directions:

Cut dowels to the right length, smoothing the cut ends with sand paper.

Drill holes through the dowel 1" and 2 1/4" from the dowel end.

Wrap the braid around the dowel, covering the drilled holes, and sew tightly together. The 1 1/2" wide braid will cover both holes, the 3/4" braid will cover one hole each.

Thread the round elastic into a needle and stitch it through the braid and a drilled hole. Stitch through the jingle loop and then back through drill hole and braid. Pull the elastic tight and knot the second jingle into it, very tightly. Repeat the same procedure for the second pair of jingles.

You may add a third pair of jingles to your own jingle stick. This will increase the sound, which is helpful in certain situations.

WILMA ELLERSIEK: A LIFE FOR RHYTHM

In a small village in Schleswig-Holstein, directly on the coastline of the Baltic Sea, on June 15, 1921, Wilma Ellersiek first saw the light of the world. With the rhythm of the waves, the murmur of the wind, and with dogs, cats, chickens, ducks and a horse as playmates, she lived a childhood bound up with nature. Her friends were, as she says, flowers, trees, sand and stars. But above all, rhythm, encountered at the seaside in many-layered forms, would stay with Wilma Ellersiek throughout her life. Looking back, she perceives her childhood as an almost heavenly life in the rhythm of nature. In her parents' home she was encouraged to pursue music, but also language and literature. Nature on one hand and culture on the other were an ideal, marvelous and edifying atmosphere for developing one's humanity.

In 1927 the Ellersiek family moved to Westphalia. Again little Wilma had the luck of living next-door to a farm; so the dear creatures remained her friends as before. New, however, was the impression of grain fields waving in the breeze, another rhythmic wave movement. Now came early meetings with other children, first in kindergarten and soon also in school. Their time together was filled with singing, dancing and recitation; indeed, looking back she sees her entire childhood and youth as suffused with music and rhythm, a sound basis for her later activity.

Wilma Ellersiek completed her schooldays with the *Abitur* examination and in 1941 she began to study in Leipzig, beginning in the major areas of school music, German philology and history of art. Serious sickness forced her to interrupt her study. This was followed by the confusion of wartime, near the end of which, in 1945, her family was forced to flee from Eastern Europe. In Essen, Wilma Ellersiek resumed her study at the

Volkwang School, albeit changing her major field. Her new field of study was rhythmic-musical education, continued in Stuttgart at the State Academy for Music and Performing Arts. There she became a student of Elfriede Feudel, herself a master student of the founder of "Eurhythmics," Émile Jaques-Dalcroze.[1] In addition to studying eurhythmics, Wilma Ellersiek also entered the study of speech education and completed both fields in 1957 with the state examination. Eurhythmics then became her life's content. She remained at the Stuttgart Music Academy as an assistant in the three departments: Eurhythmics, Theater and Spoken Word. After her time as assistant, she was offered a lecturing position, and later a professorship. In addition to her work at the Academy, she worked as stage director in opera and drama in Stuttgart, Vienna and London, among other places.

Again a serious sickness caused a decisive change in vocation, and again it was rhythm that fascinated her. Wilma Ellersiek now turned to research on the specific effects of rhythm and movement, language and music on the small child. Her work on this theme provoked attention, and in 1968 she received a research commission for it from the State of Baden-Württemberg. Out of this impulse the first "gesture-games" for the preschool child were born. Out of these little gesture-games, step-by-step, with enviable intuition, and also with enormous exactitude and care, she developed great, connected play-units in rhyme, interwoven with rhythm and music. In the beginning she called her courses "School for Parents," for her idea was to teach children together with mothers or fathers. In the late 1960's, the Stuttgart Music Academy established for Wilma Ellersiek, within the Eurhythmics Department, the specialty "Eurhythmics for the Preschool Age." During this time, a meeting took place with the "matriarch" of the Waldorf kindergartens, Klara Hattermann, with whom she maintains an intimate friendship to this day. Klara Hattermann has viewed the new games with interest, has accompanied Wilma Ellersiek through many difficulties and has encouraged again and again her continued activity. Along with several of Wilma Ellersiek's students from Stuttgart, Klara Hattermann has carried the games into the world through workshops. After twenty-five years of intensive teaching activity, Wilma Ellersiek retired, leaving the Academy in 1983. Lifted out of her teaching responsibilities, she became more creative than ever. Many of the games were developed at this time, among which are all the caresses and many lullabies. Additionally, during this time, a circle of interested friends came together in Hannover around Klara Hattermann to work intensively with the games of Wilma Ellersiek and see to their propagation in a form as true as possible to the intention of their author.

The games of Wilma Ellersiek come from her listening to Nature; in a way true to their origin she has succeeded in artistically molding speech, rhythm and the corresponding gestures to bring the wind, flowers, beasts, sun, moon and stars into the child's presence through little musical tales. In this way through the swinging, healing, natural rhythms of the games, she offers something to today's children from her own nature-filled childhood.

Ingrid Weidenfeld

---

[1] Dalcroze's Eurhythmics: not to be confused with the art of movement developed by Rudolf Steiner, called "Eurythmy."

Addresses

Waldorf Early Childhood Association of North America,
(WECAN)
285 Hungry Hollow Rd.
Spring Valley, NY 10977
Tel. (845) 352-1690
e-mail: info@waldorfearlychildhood.org

International Association of Steiner/Waldorf Early Childhood Education
PL 1800
S-15391 Järna, Sweden
Tel. 00-46-85-517-0250
Fax. 00-46-85-517-0685
Internet: www.waldorfkindergarten.de
E-Mail: geseke.lundgren@telia.com

Arbeitskreis der Ellersiek Spiele
Irmela Möller
An den Maschwiesen 2
30519 Hannover
E-Mail: s.weidenfeld@t-online.de

Lyn and Kundry Willwerth
2760 Webb Rd.
Cortland, NY 13045
Tel. (607) 756-2782
E-Mail: frauwillwerth@hotmail.com

Choroi Instruments
available at:
Rudolf Steiner College Bookstore
9200 Fair Oaks Blvd.
Fair Oaks, CA 95628
Tel. (916) 961-8729

Nova Natural Toys and Crafts
140 Webster Rd.
Shelburne, VT 05482
Tel. (802) 985-8300
E-Mail: ted@novanatural.com

Learning CDs for *Giving Love - Bringing Joy* and
Gesture Games for Spring and Summer, Autumn and Winter
available at:
Hillside Kindergarten
2760 Webb Rd.
Cortland, NY 13045
Tel. (607) 756-2782
E-Mail: frauwillwerth@hotmail.com

Gesture Games for Spring and Summer
Hand Gesture Games, Songs and Movement Games for Children in Kindergarten and the Lower Grades

By Wilma Ellersiek
Edited and translated by Kundry and Lyn Willwerth
Illustrations by Friederike Loegters
136 pages with Spiral binding.
Publisher: WECAN

Poets and musicians alike have been inspired to celebrate the renewal of spring and its fulfillment in summer.

We all know that young children show a spontaneous interest in every little ant or pebble that needs to be touched and explored. In sharing the experiences of the innumerable small wonders of nature with our children we can awaken in them feelings of love, concern and responsibility for the life of our planet.

These songs, hand gestures and movement games for the seasons of spring and summer by Wilma Ellersiek lead our children to joyful participation and understanding of nature around them.

Giving Love – Bringing Joy
Hand Gesture Games and Lullabies in the Mood of the Fifth

By Wilma Ellersiek
Edited and translated by Kundry and Lyn Willwerth
Illustrations by Friederike Loegters
110 pages with Spiral binding.
Publisher: WECAN

The first volume of Wilma Ellersiek's *Hand Gestures, Songs and Movement Games* offers lighthearted, gentle touch games for expectant mothers, parents and caregivers to play with their infants, toddlers and young children, strengthening love and confidence in the world.

These touch games, called "caresses" by Wilma Ellersiek, consist of rhymed verses or lullabies and gentle, caressing touches as were practiced in similar folk games which have fallen into disuse in today's media society.

Her lullabies are based on the experience of the fifth interval with central tone A and are often accompanied by corresponding hand gestures.